"*Science Whiz* is entertainingly told by a true 'wunderkind.' I wish I had this resource when I was in high school. A must for all would-be whizzes who want to take control of their universes."

—RICHARD STONE,
AUTHOR OF *MAMMOTH: THE RESURRECTION OF AN ICE AGE GIANT*
AND ASIA EDITOR OF *SCIENCE MAGAZINE*

"*Science Whiz* is an excellent example of how young scientists can succeed with access to the right resources. The Siemens Foundation is proud to have its author Jerry Guo as an alumni of the Siemens Competition in Math, Science and Technology. This book is full of tips and tools that students need to consider to be top contenders in science-based competitions."

—JAMES WHALEY, PRESIDENT,
SIEMENS FOUNDATION, WHICH SPONSORS THE SIEMENS COMPETITION
IN MATH, SCIENCE AND TECHNOLOGY

"Jerry Guo is an extremely smart and talented guy. The stories he's written for our magazine—from places like China and Easter Island—are as good or better than lots of stuff I get from writers with decades of experience. That's pretty impressive, considering he's 19. I'm not ashamed to predict that we'll all be working for him one day."

— IVAN ORANSKY, MD, DEPUTY EDITOR,
THE SCIENTIST MAGAZINE, ADJUNCT PROFESSOR OF JOURNALISM AT NYU AND
CLINICAL ASSISTANT PROFESSOR OF MEDICINE AT NYU

"By writing this practical and entertaining book, Jerry Guo demonstrates not only his passion for science but his commitment to helping others. Jerry leads by example encouraging other young people in the pursuit of their dreams while giving back to society in a positive manner."

—BOB AND JAN DAVIDSON, CO-FOUNDERS OF
THE DAVIDSON INSTITUTE FOR TALENT DEVELOPMENT,
SPONSOR OF THE DAVIDSON FELLOWS SCHOLARSHIP PROGRAM

"Jerry Guo's book offers an exclusive look into the world of science and gives great tips on how to get started with research. It is an essential resource for aspiring scientists, combining solid writing with accurate reporting of what goes on in science labs and how real research works. The book is a fast-paced, informative account of his successes in science and how other students can follow in his footsteps."

—DR. GISELLA CACCONE, SENIOR RESEARCH SCIENTIST
AT YALE UNIVERSITY AND DIRECTOR OF
THE YIBS CONSERVATION GENETICS LABORATORY

"This book highlights many of the fantastic opportunities and resources that are available for high school students. It's wonderful to have so many comprehensive listings complete with info bits and tips all in one place."

—SARAH LANGBERG, $50,000 GRAND AWARD WINNER AT THE INTEL INTERNATIONAL SCIENCE AND ENGINEERING FAIR IN 2004, WINNER OF $115,000 IN COLLEGE SCHOLARSHIPS AND PRINCETON UNIVERSITY STUDENT

"Jerry Guo is a clear-sighted and promising scientist. He was a superb summer student at Caltech."

—TOSHIRO ITO, PRINCIPAL INVESTIGATOR OF TEMASEK LIFE SCIENCES LABORATORY, NATIONAL UNIVERSITY IN SINGAPORE AND FORMER POSTDOCTORAL FELLOW AT CALIFORNIA INSTITUTE OF TECHNOLOGY

"This book has a plethora of helpful tips about conducting research as a high school student as well as making the most out of high school. Jerry Guo is a student who chased his curiosity, paved his own path through high school, succeeded and is now sharing his valuable insight with the world. Many opportunities that he suggested in the book—such as 'study abroad in high school' and 'take advantage of free college classes'—were things that I never thought of in high school!

"Besides being informative, this book is a fun read as well. Jerry provides rather serious advice about all sorts of dreadful things (like applying to college!), but he deftly uses a lighthearted and humorous tone, and he's not afraid to laugh at himself. He tells his life story as a kid with perpetual curiosity, genuine passion, a strong sense of drive and—above all—a sense of humor."

— LUCIE GUO, $100,000 FIRST PLACE WINNER AT THE SIEMENS WESTINGHOUSE COMPETITION IN 2005, WINNER OF $110,000 IN SCHOLARSHIPS AND HARVARD UNIVERSITY STUDENT

"Full of valuable advice and personal experience, this easy-to-follow book offers great suggestions for any high schooler passionate about science. Jerry Guo regales the reader with humorous anecdotes of gooey 'pseudo-honey' trails, cross-global travels and a 'personal Yoda,' which are especially enjoyable to read and add a colorful touch to his serious tips of what to do—or not do—to be successful with science fairs, scholarships and college applications. A great choice for the ambitious high school science student who wants to go far!"

—LISA GLUKHOVSKY, $50,000 GRAND PRIZE WINNER AT THE INTEL INTERNATIONAL SCIENCE AND ENGINEERING FAIR IN 2003, USA TODAY ALL-USA HIGH SCHOOL ACADEMIC FIRST TEAM IN 2004 AND PRINCETON UNIVERSITY STUDENT

"Why reinvent the wheel of high school research when you could just read this book? Conducting meaningful research in high school can be challenging. This book lays out a variety of useful tips and tricks that will help you initiate and carry out a successful project. Anyone wanting to get started on research while in high school stands to learn a lot from Jerry Guo."

"*Science Whiz* is at the same time very informative and entertaining. Jerry Guo has clearly laid out important lessons and tips that every high school science student aspiring to win prestigious competitions or gain entry into top colleges should know about. It would have been great to know some of these tips when I was competing in science competitions and applying to college!"

"I know from personal experience how exciting and rewarding participating in science research can be in high school. This book offers a wonderful resource, while remaining fun and innovative. I recommend it to any student looking to explore and expand upon an interest in science."

"Jerry Guo provides valuable insight on the process of applying for and succeeding in prestigious science talent search competitions. His immense success with each of these competitions gives him a rare 'inside' perspective of which strategies work and which don't. In addition, he helps form the bridge between success in high school and success in college—how to get into elite colleges by presenting one's achievements to give them the credit they deserve. Jerry's light-hearted (and at times, self-deprecating) humor holds the reader's attention throughout the book, making it an enjoyable read for all audiences—high school students, parents and budding young scientists of every type."

"This book gives an insider's view of various resources available to high school students interested in doing research. It is a fun read and the information presented is valuable."

—YUANCHEN ZHU, $50,000 GRAND AWARD WINNER AT THE INTEL INTERNATIONAL
SCIENCE AND ENGINEERING FAIR IN 2004 AND HARVARD UNIVERSITY STUDENT

"Jerry Guo's book captures how far a love of learning can take you. … I wish I had had a resource like this book when I was in high school, as it encapsulates so much information about scholarships, competitions and internships that I had to seek out on my own (and never would have found if it weren't for my mentors!) … I encourage high schoolers to use Jerry's book to help them pursue research and study in science, as it will not only help them understand the world in comprehensive and unpredictable ways, but also it can bring about academic recognition and career success."

—MOLLY FOX, USA TODAY ALL-USA HIGH SCHOOL ACADEMIC FIRST TEAM IN 2004,
AUTHOR, INTERN AT VANITY FAIR, COLD SPRING HARBOR LAB AND
YALE-NEW HAVEN CHILD STUDY CENTER AND YALE UNIVERSITY STUDENT

"I wish I had this book when I was applying for science competitions and scholarships. Jerry Guo does a great job compiling the information about the competitions. This book should be on every guidance counselor, science teacher and budding scientist's bookshelf."

—LINDSAY HAINES, 2006 USA TODAY ALL-USA HIGH SCHOOL ACADEMIC
FIRST TEAM AND YALE UNIVERSITY STUDENT
WITH A PATENT PENDING ON A WEARABLE BREAST EXAM APPARATUS

"Delivered from a charmingly personal perspective, Science Whiz provides a complete and accurately detailed guide to pursuing extracurricular academics in high school."

— BRETT HARRISON, 2005 DAVIDSON FELLOW, 2006 USA TODAY ALL-USA
HIGH SCHOOL ACADEMIC FIRST TEAM, SECOND PLACE WINNER AT THE INTEL
INTERNATIONAL SCIENCE AND ENGINEERING FAIR AND HARVARD UNIVERSITY STUDENT

"Success results when hard work meets opportunities. This book helps you maximize success by guiding you towards opportunities that you otherwise might miss."

—DAYAN LI, GRAND PRIZE WINNER AT THE INTEL INTERNATIONAL SCIENCE AND
ENGINEERING FAIR IN 2007 AND HARVARD UNIVERSITY STUDENT

"Competing in science competitions is a wonderful way for high school students to establish a work ethic, find their passion in a realm beyond high school subjects and dip their toe into the real world of professional science. In this book Jerry Guo clearly defines the intricate process required for successful science projects and highlights the terrific life and college opportunities these competitions offer their participants."

—SARAH KATE RAPOPORT, $50,000 GRAND PRIZE WINNER AT THE INTEL INTERNATIONAL SCIENCE AND ENGINEERING FAIR IN 2006, *USA TODAY* ALL-USA HIGH SCHOOL ACADEMIC FIRST TEAM IN 2006, AUTHOR OF *HISTORY'S REAL-LIFE CINDERELLAS* AND BROWN UNIVERSITY STUDENT

"This book provides useful guidance for people who are interested in any field of scientific research."

—JONATHAN CROSS, *USA TODAY* ALL-USA HIGH SCHOOL ACADEMIC FIRST TEAM AND RECIPIENT OF A FULL-RIDE SCHOLARSHIP TO DUKE UNIVERSITY WITH A PATENT PENDING ON A FUEL-CELL SYSTEM

"Let Jerry Guo guide you through the challenging transition from high school to college and through a deeper transition from complacency to curiosity. Jerry recounts the ups and downs of his forays into science with plenty of tips to learn from. He reminds us that a little curiosity can fuel the most exciting journeys."

—MARK SCHNEIDER, $100,000 FIRST PLACE WINNER IN THE SIEMENS COMPETITION IN 2003 AND YALE UNIVERSITY STUDENT

SCIENCE
WHIZ

How One Student Used Science to Get
into College and Win $100,000
in Scholarships (and You Can Too!)

By Jerry Guo
with special contributions
by Tamra B. Orr

Science Whiz: How One Student Used Science to Get into College and Win $100,000 in Scholarships (and You Can Too!)

By Jerry Guo

Published by SuperCollege, LLC
3286 Oak Court
Belmont, CA 94002
www.supercollege.com

Credits: Cover: TLC Graphics, www.TLCGraphics.com. Design: Monica Thomas Layout: The Roberts Group, www.editorialservice.com

Trademarks: All brand names, product names and services used in this book are trademarks, registered trademarks or tradenames of their respective holders. SuperCollege is not associated with any college, university, product or vendor.

Disclaimers: The author and publisher have used their best efforts in preparing this book. It is sold with the understanding that the author and publisher are not rendering legal or other professional advice. The author and publisher cannot be held responsible for any loss incurred as a result of specific decisions made by the reader. The author and publisher make no representations or warranties with respect to the accuracy or completeness of the contents of the book and specifically disclaim any implied warranties or merchantability or fitness for a particular purpose. The accuracy and completeness of the information provided herein and the opinions stated herein are not guaranteed or warranted to produce any particular results. The author and publisher specifically disclaim any responsibility for any liability, loss or risk, personal or otherwise, which is incurred as a consequence, directly or indirectly, from the use and application of any of the contents of this book.

ISBN: 1932662197

ISBN13: 9781932662191

Manufactured in the United States of America

10 9 8 7 6 5 4 3 2 1

Cataloging-in-Publication Data

Jerry Guo

    Science Whiz: How One Student Used Science to Get into College and Win $100,000 in Scholarships (and You Can Too!)
        p. cm.
    ISBN: 1932662197
    ISBN13: 9781932662191
    1. College Guides   I. Title
    2. Reference   3. Education

Contents

Acknowledgements xi

Introduction . . . How I Used Science to Get into Yale and
Win $120,000 in Scholarships 1

Section I: Senior Year 7

Section II: Lessons Learned 17

Lesson 1: *Explore Science Early and Feed Your Curiosity* 19

Lesson 2: *Pursue Your Passion Outside of School* 23

Lesson 3: *Develop Interests, Topics and Questions* 27

Lesson 4: *Enter Science Fairs* 33

Lesson 5: *Make Connections* 37

Lesson 6: *Become an Expert and Read Like Crazy* 41

Lesson 7: *Challenge Yourself in School* 45

Lesson 8: *Learn How Labs Work* 49

Lesson 9: *Consider Summer Programs and Internships and Making the Most Out of School Breaks* 53

Lesson 10: *Find a Mentor* 59

Lesson 11: *The Power of Research* 63

Lesson 12: *Do an Independent Project* 73

Lesson 13: *Publish Your Results* 79

Lesson 14: *Enter Competitions* 85

Lesson 15: *How about Summer Camp?* 97

Lesson 16: *Apply for Scholarships* 103

Section III: Timely Tips for College 117

Tip 1: *Highlight Your Projects* 119

Tip 2: *Get Recommendations* 121

Tip 3: *Make the Most of Scholarships (and More!)* 125

Tip 4: *Consider the Tech Schools* 127

Tip 5: *Hone Your Hook*   *129*
Tip 6: *Covering Your … Bases*   *131*
Tip 7: *Work at a University*   *133*
Tip 8: *Create a Resume*   *135*
Tip 9: *Enjoy the Summer after Graduation*   *139*

Appendices   **141**
Appendix A: *Research Paper*   *143*
Appendix B: *Articles*   *155*
Appendix C: *Science Organizations*   *175*
Appendix D: *Websites*   *189*
Appendix E: *Free Online Course Material*   *191*
Appendix F: *Peer-Reviewed Journals*   *195*
Appendix G: *Popular Science Publications*   *197*
Appendix H: *Books*   *199*

Acknowledgements

I would like to thank Kelly and Gen Tanabe at SuperCollege for taking the leap of faith with this project and their unrelenting support through the process. They've changed the lives of thousands of students—and now mine. To Tamra Orr for her constant patience and dedication; without her, I would still be gaming on my XPS and procrastinating on the work. To Toshiro Ito at Temasek Life Sciences Laboratory and Ylenia Chiari at Yale University for nurturing my love of research—and keeping their cool with my laboratory antics. To Gisella Caccone at Yale University for opening doors and inspiring me through her work on conservation biology. To Jan and Bob Davidson for their help in putting me through college and with the book. To Joann DiGennaro and the Research Science Institute program for an amazing summer and their support ever since. To my editor Ivan Oransky at *The Scientist* for fulfilling a lifelong dream of tracking pandas and his guidance on my writing. To my editor Richard Stone at *Science Magazine* for getting me into science writing in the first place, setting me loose around the world to wreak havoc and helping me find my voice; to Elliot Marshall for his guidance on the gene therapy story. I needed some therapy myself after that one. To my roommates Caio and Garrett for humoring me. Thanks for the memories (and photos) from our trip. To Charlotte, I owe you a platypus. Couldn't have made it through those late nights working on this without you. And I owe all my success to mom and dad; their countless sacrifices have put me at least on the path to graduating from college in five years or less.

DEDICATION

Dedicated to mom and dad

Introduction . . . How I Used Science to Get into Yale and Win $120,000 in Scholarships

The clock flashed 10:18 a.m. I had exactly 12 minutes to finish my presentation board for the local science fair, eat breakfast and actually get to the hockey rink where it was being held. The bagel on the breakfast table was the least of my worries as I frantically slapped the rest of my slides onto the board. In one fluid motion, I gracefully leapt into my mom's car, complete with my board and overflowing folder of notes. I had done it! I was basking in triumph when my mom shattered my smugness.

"Where are your pants?" she asked. I had stayed up a bit too late the night before chatting on instant messenger and I was still wearing the same comfy pair of gym shorts I had on when I had fallen into bed.

So, why was I in the car with project and without pants?

It had all started in my sophomore year of high school. Like many teens, I was very interested in tinkering with computers and surfing the Internet. And, like many of those same teens, I knew absolutely nothing about doing research or even how to write a coherent paper. That was all about to change however. And I can tell you how. But you must prepare to take an up-close and personal look at my nerdy yet fruitful life.

Let's go back to my sophomore year. I started receiving more junk emails in my "in" box. At the same time, I was taking two Advanced Placement classes, one that was about computer programming and one that was focused on statistics. On the weekends, I experimented with coding simple programs. I even did some extra credit reading on various programming techniques and statistical methods. Eventually, I put all three things together and ended up developing a new system of spam filtering. My work on that project was condensed into a few amateur slides. These were the same ones I had been busy gluing to the display board that spring morning at 10:18 a.m.

After putting on some pants and grabbing the bagel, I somehow managed to get to the science fair. Naturally, I was the last one there. To make matters worse, I realized that some of the display boards virtually blinded me with their snazzy layouts and eye-catching graphics. Mine was clearly missing snazzy layouts and eye-catching graphics.

Fortunately, this story has a happy ending. Although my display was rather crude, I managed to speak with confidence during the interviews with the judges. I knew my stuff because I had devoted much of my free time to the project. It was fun for me! After the fair, I was told that I was going to be given the opportunity to move up to the next level and compete at the Intel International Science Fair. That single decision by the judges that day opened many, many doors for me.

Three years later, I am a student at Yale University with over $120,000 of my college bill paid for by various science scholarships and awards from competitions. Since that first science fair, I've been busy, flooded with opportunities to do the things I love. I worked at the National Cancer Institute, sequencing genes that are involved in breast cancer. I also did research at the California Institute of Technology finding out how flowers develop. And that's just the beginning.

Over the last few years, I have written several news stories, primarily on wildlife conservation, for *Science Magazine*. I have participated in events hosted in fascinating places like the San Diego Zoo, Churchill Downs, the Library of Congress and even Tijuana, Mexico! I've made lifelong friends and met countless brilliant people like Colin Powell and the discoverer of the *Titanic*.

So why am I writing this book? How is it different from everything else on the shelf? Glad you asked.

Research has truly changed my life for the better in many ways that I could never have imagined. My goal in writing this book is to provide valuable information that will show you exactly how you can follow my footsteps and change your life too! When I first became interested in science and doing projects, I was shocked that I could not find a single text on how to do research or a book that gave "the scoop" on how to enter various science competitions and get scholarships. Instead, I dealt with many dead-ends and frustrating moments. THIS book is the resource that I never had but sure wished had been available!

By reading this book, you will be able to learn everything I have picked up over four years of high school, from tricks of the trade to how to use research experience to get you into a top college. I want to encourage you to at least explore the wonderful facets of research. You just might discover things you never knew about yourself and the world you live in.

Now, let's get to your question about how this book is different from the other ones stacked on the shelf about science fair projects.

- This is the only book that is geared specifically to high school students who want to pursue legitimate research, whether in a lab or as part of an independent project. There are definitely no baking soda plus vinegar experiments in here.

- This book offers an extensive and detailed list of various research opportunities, science competitions and scholarships. A list like this is unique and cannot be found in books or on the Internet.

- This book is the only book you need to guide you through the entire process of scientific research. There is no need to find, purchase and juggle separate books about writing research papers, pursuing college admissions, trying for scholarships or learning experimental design.

- Most importantly, these pages will offer you the absolute scoop on every facet of research, whether it is which summer research programs are worth your time (and which ones are all-expenses paid!) to how to get into the college of your dreams.

Who should read this book? Another excellent question. I can see why you will be a good researcher.

Do you fit any of the following profiles? If you do, this book is designed just for you.

- You have a research paper assigned but have no idea how to start it.

- You are excited about the idea of doing research after school, rather than just doing the dishes.

- You want to know how to find a research lab, a science internship or an all-expense-paid summer science program.

- You have an idea in the back of your mind that you would like to turn into a science project.

- You want to enter one of the very prestigious science competitions you've heard or read about and win one of their scholarships.

- You want to get into a top college and major in science.

Even if you cannot imagine yourself as a budding scientist, you should still read this book to expose yourself to new ideas and options down the road.

How do you use this book?

(1) **Read the book from cover to cover.** This is the best approach if you want to fully utilize the step-by-step guide on how to go about doing research in high school, from finding a project to

using your research experience to get into a top college. If you have little experience in science or are not even sure what you are getting yourself into, starting from the beginning of this book will help you make sense of this daunting new world.

(2) **Focus on the state you are currently on.** If you already have a rough idea how you want to tackle your project, just skip to the particular state or step where you find yourself now. For example, if you are already working on a project in a university lab but do not know how to effectively write up your data, read Part III on Writing and Presenting. If you just want to test the waters and are not sure if you like science all that much, read the first few chapters that explain why you should do some science research in high school and learn how to go about finding that special project that will excite your passions.

(3) **Gather background details.** This book is the only place where you will find the exclusive scoop on the most prestigious research competitions, scholarships and programs. It is the only centralized listing of research opportunities and programs that will set you on the fast track to college and a science career. It can be a very useful database for detailed listings of various competitions with critical information like how selective they are, what the awards are and the deadlines to enter each one.

However you decide to use this book, each page is jam-packed with helpful information that I could never find when I started on this wonderful journey. My deepest hope is for you to find this the perfect guide to jump-starting your own career in the sciences. I am looking forward to seeing your name in the newspaper for some fantastic discovery down the road. Best of luck and have fun!

SECTION I

Senior Year

As I tell you about how I spent my senior year, specifically my scholarship searches and college application experiences, I want you to remember something: *Do as I say, NOT as I did.* My methods were not always the best, but you can learn from my mistakes! For example, when you find yourself calling a college to find out if their deadline is Eastern or Pacific Time (because you are hoping that you might have three extra hours to write your paper), you know you waited a bit too long to get started. Trust me.

When it came to applying for scholarships and to filling out those all-important applications to college, I procrastinated a lot. However, it must be said that I *did* apply. In fact, I applied for between 15 and 20 scholarships—and I got about half of them. I should also add that I applied for both small local scholarships, as well as large national ones.

I also applied to nine schools: Harvard, Yale, Princeton, MIT, Stanford, Cornell, Clemson, Washington University and Duke. I chose Yale, Harvard and Princeton because I was really keen on a liberal arts education, especially since I was not sure what major or career I wanted at the time. I included MIT because my parents loved it, but I really didn't want to go there at all. I liked Stanford for its weather and I wanted to be near the coast. Cornell, Clemson, Washington University and Duke were schools I thought I had a good chance for being admitted, and three out of the four were pretty close to my home.

However, the reasons behind my college choices weren't truly thought out. Here is one of those places where I will recommend that you do as I say and not as I did. There are some very solid reasons for choosing which school you'd like to attend. To get yourself thinking, you can ask yourself these questions:

- **Do you want to attend a liberal arts college?** There are advantages and disadvantages for this. Take a look at some of these benefits associated with attending a liberal arts college and see if they are important factors to you:

  1. The focus is on the individual student.

  2. The classes are smaller.

3. Registration is typically easier.

4. You have better access to professors.

5. The community is often close and personal.

6. You won't get lost on campus.

7. If you need help, you won't be lost in the cracks that come from being in large classes.

8. It is easier to get involved with the campus and community around you.

Of course, with the perks come the downsides, which include:

1. MONEY—these colleges cost quite a bit more (sometimes three times more than state-funded universities!)

2. You may want a big city atmosphere with lots of opportunities, not a small town familiarity.

3. You may find less cultural diversity in the smaller colleges.

4. You won't have the chance to meet as many people.

5. There are fewer options in classes, majors and activities.

6. You could find that there aren't any major sports teams, in case that is a priority for you.

You may also want to consider these questions that are specific to science as you think about college options:

● **What kind of research opportunities would you like to have?** Some colleges are going to offer high tech labs with a lot of equipment and some will not.

● **What are your academic and career goals?** You need to look for a college that focuses on what is most important to you. Perhaps you want one that will give you access to some of the newest research technologies, equipment and experiments.

Or perhaps you'd rather attend a college that not only gives you a strong scientific background, but also a good one in the humanities and other subjects.

And don't forget to think about your general likes and dislikes when it comes to living arrangements, daily schedule, social activities and making friends. You want to be happy while you are at college so that your focus can be on studying and learning. You'll want to ask yourself these questions too:

- What kind of campus environment do you prefer? Do you want to attend a college with thousands of students or hundreds?

- Do you want to live in a modern five-story dorm or a small historical one?

- Do you want the college to be situated in the middle of a thriving, bustling city of several million people or in a small town where people recognize you when you stop in?

- Do you want to be close to home or as far away as possible?

- What kind of weather do you like best?

- Does the college offer majors that most interest you?

- What financial aid options are available to you at each college?

- What kind of academic advising/counseling does the college offer?

- What kind of reputation does this school have? Are you looking for one that has a strong academic rep? Social? Diverse?

There are so many elements to think about when choosing a college that it is foolish to rush as you assess the possibilities. Give this time and thought. Where can you find most of this information? Here are some of the best sources:

- **Read those college brochures:** These will start to come in the mail so fast you will think you are Harry Potter and Hogwarts is trying to get in touch with you. Don't just toss them in the trash. Make a file with the brochures, fliers and catalogs. Take time to read through them because you may discover facts you never knew that can help you make some decisions.

- **Check out the websites:** You already know that everything you ever wanted to know about the planet (and a lot you may have never wanted to be privy to) is on the Internet and this certainly includes college information. You can find individual sites for virtually every college, including courses offered and professor bios to student organizations and students' chat rooms.

- **Talk to current students or recent graduates:** They can tell more than any PR info. Ask them the important questions like how is the food in the cafeteria and what is the best time to grab a shower in the dorm without getting frozen or scalded. These students can give you the up-close and personal info that the brochures won't.

- **Attend college fairs and make time for visits with college reps:** The next time there is a college fair at your school or a school somewhere in your area, take the time to go and learn. Talk to as many college representatives as you can. When reps come to your school, give up your lunch hour to meet with them— yes, it's that important! Make it a priority. Even if you don't end up applying to these schools, it is a good way to learn about them and a perfect time to ask questions.

- **Look into college directory books:** These come out every year without fail and can give you amazing insight into each college. Some focus on the academics, others on majors, others on life in the dorm and still others on colleges geared for special types of students. Peruse the area in your local bookstore and see what titles pop out at you.

- **Talk to counselors, teachers and family members:** These people often have a huge amount of experience that they are just hoping you will ask them about. Talk to your parents about their college choices, if they attended college. Talk to your neighbor or the part-time guy you work with at the mall. Talk to your school counselor and your favorite teacher. The more you know, the better choices you will be able to make.

Now back to what *not* to do…don't procrastinate on writing the essays that must accompany your scholarship and/or college applications. I found the essays, together with all of the college applications, nothing short of overwhelming. I did not budget my time at all. Looking back on it, I realize that I should have planned two hours for every local application and double that for national ones. For example, with my Davidson application, not only did I have to gather recommendations and my transcript, I also had to write a 25-page paper, four—yes, FOUR essays—create a PowerPoint presentation and make a video that explained my project (the spam filter).

I was lucky. I met my goals in spite of my procrastination, although I sometimes ask myself how much better I might have done had I not waited until the last minute. Anyway, I work well under pressure and this proved it. Here is my advice: if you work at your best and are most creative when the minutes are ticking away faster and faster, do what I did. But if you only *suspect* you're good under pressure, this is NOT the time to test your theory. And if you KNOW you're lousy under pressure, don't even try it this way. Plan ahead instead.

Think about these ideas. Maybe some of them will work for you.

- Keep a special calendar in your room with all the application due dates highlighted.

- If you know how to use Excel on the computer, create a chart that lists applications, due dates, materials needed and so on. Print it out and keep it where you can see it every single day.

- Plot out how much time you need to complete each part of an application (note: it is ALWAYS, ALWAYS longer than you think. If you're planning on two hours, block out four).

- If you have to write essays, start thinking about topics and brainstorm them long before the due date. Don't start writing it the night before it is due! Remember too that you can often use the same essay for more than one application, so you want to write a quality paper that with a little tweaking can be recycled.

- If, like me, you are also required to create something like a PowerPoint presentation and/or a video of your project, you will need a LOT of time. Allow for this and use your calendar to plan times when you will work on your presentation.

- Break each application down into steps, for example, (1) learn how to use PowerPoint; (2) make an outline of what to cover and so on, and then keep a daily list so you can check off what you have and have not done. Whichever method you use to keep up, the biggest key is putting your reminder or list or calendar where you cannot miss it AND then following through with each step. Sadly, making the list isn't enough; you've got to use it.

You are going to spend the next four years of your life at a college you choose and that accepts you. This much of your life and future certainly deserves time and attention. Don't do as I did: do as I am telling you to do!

Here's the essay that I wrote to get into Yale:

PERSONAL STATEMENT

"Jerry and Me"

Many of the people who left a mark in history seemed to have names that ended with "the Great" or at least a roman numeral. In sharp contrast, I was named after the timeless mouse from the cartoon "Tom and Jerry." So would I become the ever-victorious hero like my namesake or destined for utter failure like the silly Tom?

As a wide-eyed, fun-loving preschooler in urban China, I would religiously plop in front of the small, static-plagued family television at 4:30 every afternoon for another wild adventure with "Tom and Jerry." The next half hour was the only time of the day I was not jumping around, immersed in my fantasy world where I too always defeated the feline fiend at the last second. During the commercial breaks and over the steaming aroma of dumplings wafting through the room and my mom's impatient cries that dinner would be ruined in two minutes, I diligently created out of LEGO pieces and disassembled toys scattered all across the floor the perfect scenario for my clever hero to escape from once again.

When I visited my grandma, I excitedly tried to explain about this American icon that epitomized everything I dreamed of becoming at that age (well, minus all the fur). She merely shook her head in a wise grandmotherly way with a sparkle in her eyes that said, "boys will always be boys." Indeed, in my over-imaginative mind, I was truly the dashing mouse, with a knack for pulling mischievous pranks but always managing to come out on top, thanks to quick thinking and youthful innocence.

One early morning, my grandma took me shopping for fresh vegetables at a local street market. I was fascinated by the clucking and flapping of restless chickens, the sweet scent of exotic and colorful fruits and the sizzle of tender, frying sausages. I had discovered the perfect backdrop for the showdown with my imaginary arch nemesis, the foolish yet relentless Tom. I dashed and darted between the various stalls, narrowly escaping the claws of certain doom right on my heels. Careening around a corner, I deftly dove into a pile of battered cardboard boxes, surely leaving Tom in the dust. I leapt up with a silly grin, expecting thunderous cheers for my miraculous victory.

Faced with only disapproving stares, I forged on with a spectacular finale. Spying a bulky aluminum tub filled with cold water for washing vegetables sandwiched between two counters up ahead, I climbed onto the first table, preparing to gracefully leap across the gap and leave Tom behind sputtering in the pool of water. As I sailed through the air, time seemed to stop as I basked in the glory of my most daring adventure yet. Suddenly, I realized that unless I turned into Tweety Bird, I would never make it across.

With limbs flailing, I ungracefully lunged at the counter to break my fall. The next thing I knew, cantaloupes and bananas seemed to be raining from the sky; I was also drenched with the freezing water meant for Tom's demise. Teeth clattering and knees wobbling, I crawled out of the mess physically unharmed but emotionally shaken that I, the invincible Jerry Mouse, could ever suffer such a defeat. My quick thinking couldn't bail me out this time. For the next month, I had to wash vegetables every morning in that so-called playground to compensate the vendor.

The next year I moved to America with my family. On the first day of elementary school, before I even knew the alphabet, my dad asked me if I wanted to pick an American name. Without hesitation, I immediately exclaimed, "Jerry!" Already, I knew that the playful Jerry Mouse would always be a part of who I was; however, I also realized that unlike the impish cartoon character, I would not emerge victorious in every battle. I needed to learn how to handle defeat in order to overcome the countless obstacles I would undoubtedly face in this land of opportunity. Still, every once in a while, before the rush of weekend tennis practices or debate tournaments, I would curl up in front of the television and catch another fantastic adventure of "Tom and Jerry."

Lessons Learned

Lesson 1

Explore Science Early and Feed Your Curiosity

I think that I must have been born with a fascination for science. I used to go on fishing trips with my dad but instead of fishing, I sat next to him and dissected the fish to see how it worked. I always wanted to take things apart, look at them and then find a book that told me more about what I had just seen. Fortunately, my parents supported this quality of "geekiness" about me.

My dad had a Ph.D. and he knew a great deal about science so he answered many of my questions. He had to have been very patient because I was always asking endless questions about everything around me, from the baby rabbit's nest I found in the backyard to how clouds worked. I was always excited about insects and plants and anything else in nature. We went on camping trips as a family and I wanted to know about the ecology of the wetlands, what the climate was like and so on.

I had another incredible opportunity to explore science and feed my curiosity when I was young. It is not something that everyone can do—but if you can, I HIGHLY recommend it. Hang around a university and look for opportunities to check things out and learn from what you find. I did, and it was life-changing. When I was in third grade, my parents lived in student housing. I hung out in the computer lab all the time. I tinkered around in there and no one objected because I think I was too short to be noticed. I tried hard to act older than I was. I remember the day they switched over to Windows '95 vividly because it was like a 24-hour candy shop for me. Of course, not everyone can be as lucky as I was, being able to access a university like this. But there are other ways to take advantage of opportunities around you. Some ideas for you to try include hanging out at the biggest library you can find in your area (especially if you can find one with a computer lab), shadowing a friend or family member that works in some kind of lab or following one that works in an academic environment. All of this will give you exposure to the atmosphere that surrounds science and can provide valuable information that can be a part of your future.

And don't stop with the university or college campus. Expand your fields of exploration. Go to zoos. Go to museums. Read every sign they have. If there is a presentation or a lecture, go to it. If there is a special display, see it. Watch nature shows on television. Read science magazines and books. If you are going to go on a vacation, get books about the places you will see and learn about them before you go. That way you will know what to look for and where to look to find the answers to your questions.

Keeping the passion to learn about new things is so important, no matter how old you are or how much you have learned. Just recently, I went on a trip to Costa Rica. The leader of the group knew everything there was to know about the rain forests we were walking through. We came across some leaf cutter colonies and I was just totally fascinated. I asked her endless questions: How did they consume so much so fast? How did they tend their fungus gardens? How did the ants communicate with each other? For two hours, I asked. It was just like being a six-year-old child again. I wanted to KNOW.

When I think back to what I learned in school between first and ninth grade, all I can think of is cursive writing. I learned how to sign my name really well. But everything you learn in school is fed to you—

you don't get to pursue what personally interests you. A passion for science can help you feed your interests and do it *your way*!

Lesson 2

Pursue Your Passion Outside of School

Pursuing your passion for science goes a long way beyond taking science classes in school. You have to look further than that. There are many different ways to accomplish this.

When I was in high school, I wanted to learn things that simply were not offered in any of my classes. For example, I was interested in environmental science because I had learned about a nearby water treatment plant. Since this wasn't a subject or course that was a part of my high school's curriculum, I taught it to myself. I went online and looked up other teachers' syllabi and textbooks. Then I bought the books and followed their outlines.

Next, I taught myself macro economics. I had read the *Wall Street Journal* and I wanted to know exactly what a Federal Reserve System and fiscal policy meant. I was intrigued by the subject and I found a way to learn about it.

At the time that my mom went back to college, I was in junior high. She of course was aware of my thirst for learning, so she helped me by bringing home textbooks about computers. By utilizing what my mother was able to provide to me through her own college experience, I was able to teach myself Visual Basic, C++, Html and Java.

If you want to learn about things that your school does not offer, look further.

- **Teach yourself: Get a used copy of a textbook and read it.** Check one out at the library. Ask a teacher to loan you an extra copy. Find an expert in the topic and ask him/her to teach you whenever possible.

- **Find a mentor.** We will talk about this at length later, but you can find one through work, local schools and professional organizations.

- **Take a class.** It can be at another high school, a community college or just a local class offered in the evenings or weekends. Read bulletin boards to find out about where they are and when they meet. Go to summer school. Classes are available everywhere if you just look.

- **Choose a project to investigate.** Build gadgets. Study projects others have done. Find out how things work.

- **Go outside the box.** Consider learning something that seems to be a stretch for you or outside of your comfort zone. For example, take a debate and/or speech class. You will need excellent communication skills whenever you enter a science fair.

- **Join a club or group or start one with your friends.** Who knows? You might spend the weekend building rockets. Join together to explore science.

Chances are that during your school years you have been assigned a science project for one of your classes. It is a common requirement. A mandatory science project is often not very challenging, since teachers know that you have assignments in other classes as well. But they usually vary in magnitude, from a weekend assignment of examining the contents of your refrigerator to a semester long independent project linking the school's computers into a supercomputing network.

However, one thing is for sure: what is required as a project for just one class is not an accurate reflection of real research. You are either given an experiment already conducted or designed to repeat or perhaps given specific instructions on the parameters of your project. This takes all of the creativity out of it! On the other hand, class assignments, when designed correctly, can be a tremendous catalyst that sheds new light on what science means to you. If you are interested in doing research, you should venture out of the classroom and try your hand at gaining experience in real research, whether through a university lab, corporate internship, summer program, research course or independent effort.

When I was in school, I participated in several different groups. If I could do it all over again, I think I would be involved in even more. Getting involved in extracurricular activities is, hands down, one of the best ways to get noticed when you apply for college, scholarships, internships and even jobs. Join organizations in and out of school. Learn to work with others. Learn teamwork. Learn self-responsibility. Learn the value of helping others. Not only does this help you as a human being, but it helps you as a scientist as well.

My own extracurricular experience included a time in Science Buddies, acting as a mentor to younger kids. When I was 15 years old, I volunteered in the gastrointestinal inpatient unit of a hospital. In addition, I was in the American Junior Academy of Science. That is when I started working on my spam filter project…

It was spring break in 10th grade. Life seemed boring without school, so I ended up locking myself up in my room and working on a spam filter for six days straight. Little did I know that it would take three years to complete, but I got a good start. And it all stemmed from my tinkering.

I realize that it may not be the same for you. You might not have a project that grabs your attention like I did. But somewhere inside you is the passion and you can pursue it by reading, learning, talking, listening, discovering and experimenting. When you spend enough time doing this, then you can go into the lab and because of your experience and your passion not sound . . . well . . . stupid.

Lesson 3

Develop Interests, Topics and Questions

While surfing the net in a futile attempt to avoid doing homework, I came across the site for the Dakar Rally, the race from Paris, France to Dakar, Senegal. I have had an interest in rally racing since I got my driver's license but my general lack of hand-eye coordination has held me back. I did learn how to drive a stick while I was in Costa Rica. However, that ended up being a poor choice since most of my driving took place on mountain roads—at night.

For me, rally racing was an interest at that time. I've told you that developing interests can help you further yourself in the field of science, so you might be thinking, "How could something like that be turned into a science project?" It is possible to design a meaningful project out of almost any field of interest. And if you base your projects on your personal passions, you are more likely to follow through with them and not lose interest when you are only a few days into the planning.

Let's look at where my interest in rally racing might take me, for example. I started with an interest and by focusing on one that I wanted to explore, I have created a topic. Because of my background in computers and robotics, the part of rally racing that would be particularly interesting to me is autonomous (driver-less) driving. The U.S. military has been working on autonomous technology for years and has even deployed autonomous aerial drones for surveillance missions over Iraq and Afghanistan. Their research branch, DARPA, has been funding a sexy but cutthroat rally race from Los Angeles to Las Vegas for autonomous vehicles for the last three years. First place? $2,000,000!

Once you have gone from an interest to a topic, it is time to turn it into a central question. This is what your project will focus on. From the topic of autonomous vehicles, I might decide to look into finding out how the on-board computer could recognize a rock. This might seem somewhat trivial, but the question actually has several layers. First, how would a computer capture visual signals? Would it use visible light, infrared or radar? Would the system use a variety of cameras and how would the various inputs be combined? Once there was a picture, how does it decide what constitutes a rock? In other words, the computer will need to know the difference between a rock and a shrub.

For some projects, a question may not be necessarily the right approach. Often, a project may be to develop a particular gadget or to improve a system. In these instances, the question turns into more of a "goal." During my sophomore year of high school, I got fed up with the amount of junk email I was bombarded with and decided to develop my own spam filter. I was not interested in answering a question but in creating something. Still, the filter was the outgrowth of my interests.

Recognizing Your Interests

Start reading magazines and newspapers, browse the Web or watch television—nowadays there are plenty of sources to get news about science. Immerse yourself in the current pulse of research and scientific developments, as you likely want to work on a topic that is considered to be important.

Next, keep track of what kind of articles pique your interest. You may find that you have eclectic interests or that you gravitate towards articles within a discipline such as biology. Don't be afraid to walk your own path though. Working within a field that is "hot" may be especially convenient if you spend a summer doing research in an institution or university, since the infrastructure and protocols have already been established by previous researchers.

If you want to develop a meaningful project on your own, your interests may not jive at all with those of academic researchers. To maintain those personal interests, keeping up with the news is a good start. Go beyond the research printed or discussed—dig deeper and see if you can develop your interest into a topic or question that is outside of the standard science paradigm.

The real trick to making sure you have a solid and valid project is to find a mentor or advisor, ideally someone who works in the same field. Your mentor will be an invaluable resource in keeping your project afloat. At the same time, he or she will make sure that you remain grounded and on track. You will most likely get stuck on something in your project and at those times, an outside perspective is just what you need to get going again.

I really lucked into my main project in high school. Growing up, I had countless—often unrelated—interests. From safari animals to chemistry sets, my mind was all over the place. While I was in middle school, my mom went back to school to get a computer science degree. She brought home books with brightly colored covers and titles like *Operating Systems* or *Data Structures*. I flipped through some of her books and found one that covered introductory Visual Basic, a nifty programming language that allows a person to make simple form-based programs.

I became more and more interested in computers and technology, especially as the Internet exploded and waves of new startups became overnight sensations. When my sophomore year came around, I decided to take a programming class. At the same time, I began to receive more and more junk emails, which helped me to narrow down my interest to a topic: spam filtering.

Narrowing Down to a Topic

Once you have recognized your interests, it can be bewildering to know what to focus on for an official project. A good way of zeroing in on a potential topic is to check out what everyone else is working on or at least what people are talking about. Back in high school, there was quite a bit of buzz about spam filtering and all the hotshots in the tech world were churning out spam filters. Yahoo, Hotmail, AOL, Norton and Symantec all had products and services to combat junk email. When a herd of people are working on something, chances are the payoffs are pretty good—or at least it is something with the potential of being interesting!

Another approach for finding a good topic is to think about problems, nuisances or fields that could use improvement. For instance, it is still hard for villagers in developing countries to have access to clean water at a cheap price. It might be straightforward to ship in a high-tech distillation or reverse-osmosis unit, but it is another thing to offer a solution that is affordable for the average villager. If you are interested in sustainable development or conservation, perhaps water purification could be your topic.

The topic for my project came up naturally because the explosion of junk emails was a problem that hit me personally head-on. I felt like, if nothing else, tinkering with spam filtering might mean less wasted time deleting messages on the computer.

Picking a Question

One of the biggest dangers with science projects is not having an exact question or goal in mind from the start. When you are in the middle of a project, it is hard and frustrating to start from scratch because you realize you did not design the experiment correctly or that you did not ask the right questions. Knowing what constitutes a good question or a bad question (or worse, not having any question in mind at all!) can mean the difference between clean data and a nightmare.

It is easy to make the mistake of confusing a topic with a question. A topic that is not specific enough will usually be unsuccessful. You will end up trying to take on what could easily turn out to be someone's life work. For instance, the topic of cancer is something that thousands of researchers are working on at this very moment. Even a narrower topic like breast cancer metastasis is a huge topic when you think about the number of people working on it. Another reason it is dangerous to start a project with a topic but no question is that you will inevitably go off into countless different directions and lack focus.

The best questions are the most specific ones. Questions that examine one aspect of a phenomenon will keep your project manageable and help you zoom in on clean results that show some sort of impact.

But in some fields, a question is not particularly appropriate. For projects in engineering, for example, you might have a goal instead. For example, the first goal of my spam filtering project was to use a novel method (in this case, statistics) to develop a system that could learn over time what I considered spam versus legitimate email. The second goal was to have accuracy as high as what a human could manually filter. This meant catching 99 percent of junk emails but, at the same time, maintaining a very low false positive rate or accidental deletion of legitimate emails.

As you can see, just being interested in a topic is the first step in developing a viable project. It is vital not to stop there, though. From your interest, you need to create a topic and then focus on an element as you narrow things down to a question or goal. Sound like fun? It is. Just imagine: Who knows what this pathway may lead you to discover?

Lesson 4

Enter Science Fairs

Science fairs are a true high school phenomenon. They can be incredibly educational and even a lot of fun. I was in three of them myself. In 10th grade, I was in the regional Intel Science Fair, often referred to as "The Big One." I advanced on to the international level, where, among thousands of contestants, I took third place in the computer science division. In 11th grade, I was in the South Carolina division of the American Junior Academy of Science Fair; and in my senior year, I was in the Junior Science Humanities Symposium Science Fair.

I learned a great deal about science fairs during my high school years. Let me share some of that information with you:

Science fairs are typically held in the spring. Everyone who participates either brings a poster board, or more recently, the three-paneled boards that are available now. When I went, I made mine out of three pieces of plywood, painted black and then joined together with hinges. You want your poster board to have the right appearance. It is very important to your success. You need pizzazz. You need sparkle. Use borders. Use colors. Use pie charts, graphs and photographs. The more, the better, when it comes to visual elements.

Make sure that your presentation board is big enough to attract attention—you want people to be able to read your poster from six feet away. However, don't *overdo* your board. If you put too much on it, it will look cluttered. It is better to be simple and clean. Also give it a title—the snazzier the better. My spam filter project was "Slam the Spam." You can follow the title with a subtitle that scientifically explains what your project is truly about—but it is the snazzy title that will catch people's eyes and make them want to know more.

Beyond the graphics and title, the display board should be a user-friendly cross between a PowerPoint presentation and research paper of your project. In other words, it should have enough of the details to give scientists in the discipline a sense of what you accomplished, but condensed enough to go through in just a few minutes (hence like PowerPoint).

The best way to make the display board is actually to use PowerPoint: you can either treat each panel as a series of PowerPoint slides, or print the display board as one very large slide (the dimensions of the page in PowerPoint are adjustable). Imagining your display board as a printed-out presentation is also good because it'll help you avoid the number one flaw with display boards: trying to cram too much in.

Here are the essentials you should include; but remember, keep it simple:

- Abstract
- School / grade / any mentors
- Brief intro; bullets are good
- Hypothesis / goal
- Very brief methods; bullets or lists here are particularly effective
- Results, usually in the form of graphics, but including at least a paragraph of text summarizing the data
- Discussion/conclusions combined; keep it to bullet points or very short sentences, definitely not rambling sentences.

Many of the displays include a PowerPoint presentation with them. They feature a short introduction, as well as the methodology used, results and conclusions. You want to keep actual words to a minimum and what is there should be in print large enough to read from several feet away. It helps to have something in your display that people can hold, touch or manipulate. It draws them to your material, and something tangible helps to reinforce your message when they interact with it.

Judges commonly come by your display while you are not there. They look over everything, and then they return later to listen to your three-to-five-minute explanation of your project. These judges are usually parents and other educated people rather than experts. In a science fair, YOU are the expert on your topic. You know it better than anyone else. In those few moments, you have to sell your project, explaining it in terms everyone can understand.

Usually the judges will ask you some basic questions like these:

- What part of the project was the most difficult?

- How did you come up with the idea in the first place?

Then they will ask questions that are more specific to your project.

Here's what the judges asked me about my spam filter:

- Why did you decide to develop your own spam filter?

- How much help did you get? And on what?

- What are the advantages of your spam filter versus AOL or Yahoo's?

- What still needs to be improved or worked on?

They also asked some specific statistical questions and a couple of questions about why I chose to display the data in a particular way.

You should be prepared for a bevy of questions that will span the gamut of your research. To answer them, you will need to know every detail of your project inside and out. You are there to show why what you did is important, what you learned and how you did it.

Typically, you should provide all of the following in your oral presentation:

- Title

- Your name

- How you got interested in the project and your reason for choosing it

- Your purpose/what you were trying to discover with the project

- Exactly how much help you received, so judges know how much of the project is "your own"

- The procedure you used in a logical, step-by-step manner

You will want to show confidence when you present your project. (Remember: You are the expert!) Here are some tips:

- Use a pointer so you can point to different elements of your poster without having to stand in front of it.

- Explain your results.

- State your conclusion and freely admit any limitations you had—judges respect this.

- Ask the judges for any questions they have and answer them to the best of your ability.

In the weeks leading up to the science fair, take time to practice your presentation often. You want it to sound smooth and comfortable, not stilted and nervous. On the day of the fair, you want to dress neatly, stand up straight, speak loudly enough for all to hear you, not chew gum and make eye contact with the judges. This is your 15 minutes of fame, so make the most of it.

Lesson 5

Make Connections

Have you ever heard the expression, "It's not WHAT you know but WHO you know?" There is truth to that in many aspects of life and that includes pursuing an education and career in science. Taking the time to make connections with people is important—and it will most likely give you a tremendous head start!

So how do you go about meeting knowledgeable people and learning from quality resources? You have to know where to look. Here are some suggestions:

(1) **Attend lectures.** If your school, local university or any other organization is hosting any kind of educational lecture, go to it. Even if it is not in a field that you particularly like or understand, give it a try. You might find an all new passion. Check local bulletin boards in bookstores, libraries and schools. Often they are announced in the local newspaper. If there is a college in your town, you might find that appearances by guest lecturers are listed there. Public broadcasting radio stations and television channels often promote them as well.

(2) **Go to conferences.** Again, watch for announcements in your school, local bookstores and so on. Check bulletin boards wherever you go. Although most of these conferences tend to have a cost of some sort, check to see if there are special discounts for students.

(3) **Join national organizations.** Go online and find national organizations in your field of interest. Look into joining them. See if they have regional or local meetings. Find out if they can connect you with other members in your community. Also look at the back of this book for resources.

(4) **Talk to teachers.** Believe it or not, teachers can be a great resource to people, even those who are outside their immediate field of study. You may think your history teacher only eats, breathes and lives history, but perhaps her brother/uncle/neighbor/cousin is a lab researcher. Let your teachers know the area you are most interested in studying and see if he/she can hook you up with some other link.

(5) **Find other students.** Connect with other students who are looking for someone to share their interest in science. You can post something on the school bulletin board or in the school newspaper. Let the word out that you want to get a club started to build rockets, work with ham radios, make robots or whatever you want to try. In my case, I wanted to learn how to brew homemade beer. Since I was under age, I brought in a couple of older friends to help me. I wanted to make beer, not drink poison. We made a combination of ingredients and put it in a five gallon white tub with a metal handle. We left it for a couple of weeks and then took a leap of faith. It wasn't half bad.

(6) **Email experts.** Don't let names in print scare you. Just because someone has written an article or a book does not mean they are superior and inaccessible. If you read something that impressed or inspired you to know more, contact the author.

You might have to do it through the book or magazine publisher, but sometimes they will forward your message to the author who then has the choice to contact you. Often, the author will respond and you have the opportunity to discuss the finer points of the article. If you read a scientific paper, contact the researcher who wrote it through the organization or university. Don't be intimidated by any of these people. Most of them will likely feel honored to hear from you. Let them know why you admire their research and how it relates to your own field of interest. You may be their very first "groupie."

(7) **Take community college classes.** You do not have to be limited to taking only high school classes. Look into what your local community colleges offer. If you see a class that intrigues you and it is offered in hours where you are not in regular school, sign up. You may meet teachers and other students there who can help support your interests.

(8) **Go to the library.** Your school or public library can lead you to additional resources, including books, movies and publications. Be sure to talk to the librarians themselves. They often are familiar with local resources and may be able to connect you with someone.

(9) **Consult your counselor.** Make friends with your counselors. If they like you and see your sincere interest in learning more, they will bend over backwards to help you. They often have more connections with the community than anyone else in the school, so get to know them.

(10) **Go net surfing.** You already know that the Internet is the searcher's best friend, regardless of what you are actually searching for. This is true here as well. Play around with putting different words in the search boxes of some of the major search engines. See if you can find up-to-date

information on upcoming lectures or conventions, local authors and much more.

(11) Read the newspaper. You may typically only check the comics and the sports scores, but look a little further at some of the community listings. Watch for announcements about groups, clubs and other activities that you might want to be part of and make some of those connections.

(12) Visit a university. If you have any college or university nearby, visit. Check out the library. It has more technical reference material than the typical library. In addition to the library, try meeting some of the professors there. Visit the department you have the most interest in and meet some of the staff. They are some of the best resources you will find.

Remember to have paper and pen (or Blackberry) in hand when you pursue any of these options. You are out there to meet people and make connections, so don't blow it by forgetting names, email addresses and phone numbers. Write them down somewhere safe and then use them when the chance comes up. These are the people who can help connect you to lab work, internships, classes, expeditions, books, organizations and everything else. Praise their work and let them know that they have made an impression on you.

Explain your own interests and what you are hoping to achieve in your future education. When you speak again with one of these people, you can ask them for their guidance, suggestions or advice. Do they know of an internship or lab that might be a good fit for you? Is there a colleague you should meet? Is there a way to set up a job shadowing or a tour of their lab? And always, *always* thank them sincerely for their help and their time. They are important to you. You gotta have connections!

Lesson 6

Become an Expert and Read Like Crazy

R ead books, magazines, professional papers, newspapers—whatever you can that will show and teach you more about science. Where can you find information to read that is pertinent to your specific scientific interests? I love it when you ask me that. Here are some possibilities to explore:

(1) **Read Internet forums.** As you well know, you can find almost ANYTHING on the net. Check to see if there is some kind of forum about the scientific aspect you like most. What are people talking about? Ask questions: Can they recommend a site, book, organization or other resource? Just reading their conversations can help you understand jargon, slang and other inside tips. Check out major science sites like the National Academy of Sciences (www.nasonline.org) for updates and news as well.

(2) **Read professional papers.** See if you can find professional papers on the net that you can read. In the beginning, the terminology might be a tad overwhelming but don't give up

and go back to reading "manga." You may not be a researcher, but you are working on becoming one. Remember the affirmation, "To become, act as if." This simply means that if you want to become something (thinner, smarter, richer, etc.), act as if you already are. By adapting those habits, your chances of achieving your goal will go up.

(3) **Do your own literature review.** One of the things many researchers do to prepare for a new avenue of research is to read as many papers on the subject as possible. They also do something that most readers don't—they go to the end of the article or the back of the book and they look up each and every reference listed there. Then they read those papers and those books and so on. This is often referred to as a "literature review." You will soon start to find that the papers/books begin to circle back to each other, an indication that you have read most of what is out there.

(4) **Put the library to work.** Have you ever gone to the library for a resource and it isn't there? Another copy may be at a different branch—or it may be several states away.

Don't stop there. Ask for an interlibrary loan form (some are in hard copy and some are on the net at the library's site). Fill it out and the library will get that book for you, usually at a low cost or even no cost.

(5) **Check out the local bookstores.** Go to your local Barnes & Noble, Borders or other bookstore and spend time looking at the new nonfiction titles. What do you see that sparks your interest? If you are not sure, take a look at the nonfiction bestseller's list before you go. What is there that sounds like a possibility? Recently I read Jared Diamond's *Guns, Germs and Steel*, which was fascinating. Now I am reading his next book, *Collapse*. Scan the shelves and pick out something that will stretch your brain a bit.

(6) Subscribe to magazines and newspapers. Recently, I was reading in a magazine about a man named Dominique Gorlitz who is getting ready to set out across the Atlantic Ocean in a primitive reed boat to test out a theory he has. (Read more at www.stonewatch.de/media/download/WWRockArtNews-GB.pdf) That brought up questions in my mind as well as a memory of a similar story about Robert Ballard, the man who initially discovered the Titanic. He is basically the underwater version of Indiana Jones. I read a great deal about him and eventually got to meet him. That was a moment I will never forget.

Read magazines and newspapers—better yet, subscribe to them so you can keep on the cutting edge of technology and research. I recommend everything from *Popular Science, New Scientists* and *Discovery* to *The Scientist, Time* and *National Geographic.*

The only way to know what research is being done and reported, what research is being done that is slipping under the radar and what research is not being explored is to read and keep up with the changes. In pursuing a career in science, it is a must!

Lesson 7

Challenge Yourself in School

School is great. It's very important. A quality education is even more important and when it comes to getting one, it may mean that you need to think outside the box a bit or, in this case, think outside the school.

Classes are good, teachers are skillful—but when you think about it, most everything that you are learning is being fed to you. Your teachers, as well as the administration and governmental influences like the "No Child Left Behind" movement, determine what you do and do not learn in the classroom. But that does not have to be the entire sum of your education. I strongly encourage it not to be, in fact.

What else can you do other than go to school every day? What a coincidence. I happen to have a list for that right here.

(1) **Take AP classes.** If advanced placement classes are available at your school, take them. I took biology, chemistry, physics, U.S. history, European history, English literature, calculus, computer science, statistics and Spanish literature. This will not only help you with finding a possible passion in the sciences, but AP courses also add weight to your college admissions forms when you list them there. Colleges like to

see that you are not taking the easy route and are academically prepared for college-level courses.

(2) **Convince your school to let you take independent projects.** For more information on independent projects, check out the chapter in this book on them. If you have good grades and your counselor, as well as other staff, knows you well, you may be able to convince them to let you create/design your own project and complete it in your own time. Don't go to the staff, however, until you have figured out exactly what you would like to do and how you would like to do it. Vagueness won't win you any points. Have an outline. Bring in the sources you would use. Talk about who you would use as mentors. Make a good impression.

(3) **Take an online course.** There are a LOT, I mean, A LOT of online courses you can take. Just put "online college/high school courses" in the search box and prepare to be deluged. Bring a sack lunch before you log on. It will take you a while. One particularly great online school is the Stanford EPGY program (http://epgy.stanford.edu) which gives you credit for taking online courses through Stanford—on such essential subjects such as calculus and physics.

(4) **Buy and study your own textbooks.** Check out my other chapters and you will see I mention this. If you like a certain course that your school does not teach, look elsewhere. Check community colleges. Go online. If nothing else, find a high school somewhere in the country that is teaching this, contact them for information on what textbook and syllabus they use and then imitate it. Buy the book, follow the syllabus and learn the topic at home on your own time.

(5) **Take advantage of FREE college classes.** Yes, I meant to say FREE. There are a number of colleges that offer free online classes. Just to get acquainted with the idea, I recommend you check out http://ocw.mit.edu/index.html. This lists

MIT's free courses that you can take—the perfect place for an aspiring scientist to start.

(6) **Find a class at another high school.** Bet you had never thought of that! When I was in high school, I wanted to take a course in Spanish literature that some of my other friends were taking at their school. Why? I have NO idea. Sure, I had been taking Spanish for three years, but my handle of the language was shaky even for ordering Mexican take-out. So I arranged to take the class at a high school a few miles away from mine. I drove from my school to the other one, took the class and then had seven minutes to drive back, park and get to my next class. If you want to do this, talk to the administration. Follow earlier instructions though. Be concrete about what class you want to take and how and why you are going to accomplish it.

(7) **Go to community college.** Community colleges often offer fascinating and higher level classes than you will get in high school. Find out what is offered during the hours you are not in high school and sign up. You will meet some interesting classmates, learn new material and maybe even make some connections through the college staff.

(8) **Attend summer school at local universities.** A number of state colleges and universities offer summer school classes. When you have a free summer in front of you, learn to make the most of it. Use that time to take courses that you find interesting and that will further your science career. Make some of those important connections while you are at the college or university taking classes.

(9) **Study abroad for high school if possible.** Some high schools will offer you the chance to study abroad for part or all of the year. If that sounds like something you would like to pursue, talk to your counselor as well as your parents. It is a big step but

it can be an incredible experience. Find out more about it at www.studyabroad.com/highschool.

(10) **Take outdoor programs in your area.** It is easy to fall prey to only thinking about taking science, science, science, but there are other types of education that can end up indirectly supporting your passion for science. For example, try taking some outdoor programs that could teach you about nature (which is as scientific as you can get!) as well as about yourself.

Remember that your education is up to YOU, not your school. They provide material to you and it is up to you to learn it. It is equally up to you to realize that sometimes that is not enough and you need more. That is when you look outside your school's four walls and see what else the world has to offer. It's a big planet—don't miss out on any possibility that might come your way.

Lesson 8

Learn How Labs Work

Working in a lab is one of the best parts of being a scientist. Knowing how it works and what to expect makes it even better. Let's start with what NOT to do in a lab.

My first day in any lab, I somehow manage to make a fool of myself. I don't mean to—it just happens. Maybe you can learn from my mistakes.

Lesson 1: Do not leave important things out in the lab.

When I was working at the National Institutes of Health, I accidentally left an enzyme out overnight. Now, enzymes are very reactive. If they are left out, they do not just sit there. They, well…start *reacting*. By morning, it was pretty much all used up. The postdoc (postdoctoral fellow) I was paired with was very angry with me; but instead of just saying "I am soooooo sorry," I jokingly said, "Don't worry; I'll pay for it." This tiny little enzyme about the size of a thumb ran about $500. So . . . maybe not.

Lesson 2: Don't water the boss's desk.

Later—after duly groveling about the enzyme fiasco—I was asked to fill up a tank with chemicals. It was located above my supervisor's desk.

I didn't realize that the nozzle on the bottom of the tank was open; so as I filled up the tank, it gushed out and flooded his desk.

Lesson 3: Don't oversleep.

The night before I started working in the lab at Caltech (California Institute of Technology), I went out to dinner with my postdoc. I wanted to make a good impression on him. When he said goodnight, he said "See you at 9." Naturally, I had to top that so I replied, "I will be there at 8:30." I went home and went to bed. The next morning I woke up with a terrible feeling. You know that sinking feeling in your stomach when you just KNOW that something is wrong? I looked at the clock. It was 1:00 in the afternoon. I went into the lab and there was just nothing for me to say. We ended up laughing about it all at the end of the semester, but I will never forget that moment when I woke up and realized that I had overslept.

Lesson 4: Wear the right clothes.

The morning our lab team was leaving for Galapagos, I showed up at 7:30 a.m. at the lab. Despite repeated emails telling me what to wear, I picked out the wrong outfit. I had to strip down to my underwear and switch pants in front of the professor, a woman who clearly excels at the art of keeping a straight face. It was the first day I had met most of the team. How was that for a great first impression?

Okay, avoid those things. Here is some better advice.

I have personally worked in three labs so far. The first one was at Caltech following my junior year. It was a genetics lab. We studied flowers. *Yes, flowers*. It may not sound very exciting, but it was. Our research focused on a mustard weed that is like the lab rats of plants (if you could make the comparison between flowers and rodents).

My second experience was at a genetics lab at the National Institutes of Health. I worked there the summer after my senior year. I got in by literally sitting down and emailing over 2,000 people who worked there. I cut and pasted for hours. From that, I got ten offers and was able to pick the one I preferred. The lab I ended up in was investigating breast cancer.

After my freshman year at Yale, I worked in an ecology lab that worked on issues like molecular systematics, genetic conservations and DNA fingerprinting. We were literally piecing together elements of evolution. I worked with giant tortoises from the Galapagos Islands and geckos from Madagascar, while others worked with Siberian tigers or marine lizards.

Now, on to what a lab is like.

A lab is a fantastic place to be. The work is often diverse and fascinating. There are multiple languages spoken and different foreign talents. Often being part of a lab team means you get to do some exotic traveling.

There is a definite hierarchy in a lab. The boss is the P.I. or Principle Investigator. He is always a Ph.D. and it his job primarily to write grants and attend conferences. This is the person who comes up with the initial idea that everyone will spend their time experimenting with.

The next level is lab technicians. They usually have a Master's degree and are also full-time staff members. They do some simple experiments but it's not like they are there to do dishes.

Postdocs are next. "Postdoc" is short for postdoctoral fellow. Postdocs are Ph.D. recipients who are accepted into fellowship programs that give them opportunities to do research and perhaps even pursue careers at that university. They are in the lab for two to three years on average. Sometimes, they are not permanent but while they are in the lab, they build up their resumes and publish papers.

If the lab is university based (rather than governmental), the next level is graduate students. They are there working on their Ph.D.s and generally stay for four to six years. They sometimes rotate from one university lab to the next one.

Finally, there are the undergraduates and high school students, which could be loosely categorized as "interns." If you present well, there is a university in your area and you are willing to commit a year to helping in the lab, you may get a start as a high-schooler. It is often just a 9 to 5 job, Monday through Friday, but it is a great experience that looks terrific on your resume. Being in a lab truly does open doors to many colleges.

Laboratory experiences are often available through universities, non-profit research centers, governmental agencies and private companies. Small labs are nice because they are intimate and the P.I. is usually young and accessible. Large labs, on the other hand, often have the most high-tech equipment and more people to work with, but you may never get to speak to the P.I.

Another source to check out is the website www.collegeconfidential.com because there are discussions about lab opportunities there as well. And don't wait until April to start looking like . . someone . . . did. Instead, start in January. You will have a much better chance of getting in that way!

Lesson 9

Consider Summer Programs and Internships and Making the Most Out of School Breaks

Summer vacation and spring breaks may seem like the perfect time to sleep in, stop reading and do nothing more energetic than work the television remote; but if you want to really experience science, you need to make the most of these precious weeks. Here is what I have done for the last few years:

2004: Summer following my Junior year in high school: I worked at Caltech. (I've already told you all about that and don't want to bore you by going through it again.)

2005: Summer following my Senior year in high school: I worked at NIH (ditto parenthetical remark above).

2006: This one was a busy summer. I managed to go to China, London and the Galapagos islands. Want to know more? Let's look at China first. I went there to write a story for *Science Magazine*. I had emailed the editor who covers Asia and sent my resume and clips (copies of published articles). The editor decided to give me a go mainly because I knew Mandarin and had lived in China. I did a number of stories about science, including a profile of a high school research program in Shanghai and an investigative report of the Chinese gene therapy industry. I also went panda hunting and toured the Three Gorges Dam. For one of the trips, I even got to go with my college suitemates. Obviously, I learned about the topics I was researching, as well as how to survive in another country without a tourist guidebook. I loved traveling with my friends but did not enjoy the logistics of trying to do 18 things in two weeks.

After China, I went to London. I had heard about an internship program through my school called Bulldogs in Britain. I sent in my resume and did a phone interview, winning a spot in that internship program. I really wanted to try working in a different country for the summer, especially one in Europe. While I was there, I worked at a law firm on a book project titled, *Road after Rhodes*. It was about female Rhodes Scholars and their successes and challenges after Oxford. While I was a part of this program in London, I learned about office dynamics, plus how to live on my own away from home.

Finally, I went to Galapagos. To make this happen, I emailed a bunch of Yale professors who were conservationists. I asked them if I could tag along with them to do fieldwork. I also applied for a Yale grant, which I got. While I was there, I wrote another article for *Science,* this time about the archipelago's goat problem. I was so excited to go there because it had always been a dream. I have a fetish for islands but hey, the Galapagos is a biologist's paradise. While I was there, I collected blood samples for a genetic diversity study of giant tortoises. I learned about the biology of the Galapagos, how field work works and about invasive species. The best part of the experience was being able to camp out and search for and handle giant tortoises every day. The worst part had to be pushing our SUV through the mud and carrying all the gear for forever, including very, *very* heavy water jugs.

- **2006-7:** During the winter, I went to Costa Rica. I had received an email about a bat course…you know, the kind that fly. I was intrigued by the thought of spending time in a rainforest, plus studying bats seemed like a once-in-a-lifetime opportunity. So I filled out a standard study-abroad application and was accepted. While I was in Costa Rica, I captured different kinds of bats and learned how to identify them. I also did a small project on host-parasite dynamics, or bat flies. The best part was breathing the incredibly fresh air of the rainforest and the worst was definitely the mosquitoes.

- **2007:** During spring break, I went back to China for the second time. I went to track pandas for a story in *Science* about their recent comeback in the wild. This time I took a photographer friend along to take pictures for the story.

As you can see, my summers and school breaks were a little more exciting than being a couch potato. I have future plans in the works for a trip to Easter Island as my next trip.

So how do you get started if you want to travel during the summer or at least get yourself into some kind of summer internship? Here are my suggestions:

- **Go net surfing.** Put "high school summer research" in the search box and see what comes up. For example, the Research Science Institute is a summer research program that is a good fit for high school students during the summer after the junior year. It is held at MIT and around Harvard. Another possibility is NASA's Sharp Program, plus the government has national labs like Los Alamos and Oak Ridge who accept high school students. Go online to find the applications. Most of these programs do not pay you for your time but all of your expenses are covered.

- **Think small.** Look into some of the smaller places that do not necessarily have any internship listings. You can email them and simply ask if you can help or tag along on a project. You will not get paid, but may be able to go each day after school. You will learn a lot!

- **Look for colleges and universities.** If you live anywhere near any colleges or universities, contact them to see if they have programs that need assistants or interns. Often these places will actually pay you for your time.

- **Start early.** Ideally (this is a "Do as I say, not as I do" moment), start looking for programs in the fall. When you find five to ten places that intrigue you, send emails introducing yourself and explain how you want to learn more about science. In January, follow up with a resume and start asking how you might get involved. By March, you should have a summer internship all lined up.

- **Be creative.** Often the best way to find an internship possibility is by looking up the profiles of projects and scientists on the web and then directly contacting the person(s) in charge. Don't wait for an application to come to you or an internship to be organized, but talk directly to the postdoc in charge and get some kind of verbal agreement.

- **Design your own program.** If you cannot find what you are looking for, consider putting together your own kind of program. For example, a friend of mine just came back from a small place in Africa where he shot exotic birds to bring back for a museum to examine and put in their collections. He came up with the idea by himself and presented it to the museum.

- **Work for "the man."** You can also find internships at individual companies. Places like Siemens and Microsoft often hire interns for the summer. Look online to see if the company's website lists who to contact. If not, call the general number and ask.

- **Go outside.** Look into summer trips like the types offered by organizations such as Outward Bound (www.outwardbound. org) or the National Outdoor Leadership School (www.nols. edu). They can teach you very important skills as well.

- **Mind the gap.** Go online and put "gap year" or "summer break trips" in the search box. What comes up? You can find summer job opportunities that are paid, as well as volunteer positions in and out of the country. Suggested sites include www.gapyear.com or www.gap-year.com/browse2. asp?catID=1155. These will get you started.

One question does come up with all of these possibilities since the majority of them require that you pay for at least the transportation to and from the internship or research site: Where do you get the money?

Once you are in college, funding your research trips is easier. There are usually grants and summer funds for students. While you are in high school, however, it is tougher. I recommend that you look into local grants and scholarships through your school, your parent's employment or local professional organizations or societies. Learn how to write your own grant proposals and turn them in to the right places. Get a part-time job and ask for financial aid. This kind of experience is worth it.

The truth is this: if you are a bright high school student with a genuine passion for science, there are places that want your help and enthusiasm. You just have to put some effort into finding them. Believe me—I've been there, done that—it is worth every second you spend working for it.

Here's the email that helped me find a research position at the National Institutes of Health. I literally sent this email to 2,000 employees, received 10 offers and eventually selected work at a genetics lab researching breast cancer.

To: name@nih.gov

From: Jerry Guo

Subject: Summer research opportunities

Greetings,

I am very interested in your research and if possible, I would like to work in your lab this summer. As a rising freshman at Yale, I am currently first in my senior class with a 1600 on the SAT. I spent last summer conducting research under the head of the biology department, Professor Elliot Meyerowitz, at Caltech on gene expression of flower development. I have also worked on machine learning with Oak Ridge National Laboratory. Please let me know if there are any opportunities available in your lab or through the Summer Internship Program in Biomedical Research (application on file). Thank you for your time and consideration.

Jerry Guo

Lesson 10

Find a Mentor

One of the best ways to make connections, learn new ideas, discover new possibilities and make friends is through finding mentors. I know it has helped me a number of times.

My first mentor was a person who hardly even knew me. I was in high school and there was this guy named John. He was a legend at my school. He supposedly "cured cancer" as a junior and won a lot of scholarships. I remembered the names of some of the scholarships that he was rewarded, for example, the *USA Today* All-USA Academic Teams, and I applied for them also. Even better, I won them as well. He was my mentor in that he showed me what was possible and how to reach those goals. I met with him a few times and he was pretty genuine too.

Another mentor was a man named Toshiro, my postdoc at Caltech. He was a rather short guy and I am 6'4", so we made an odd couple. He was like my own personal Yoda—a very small, wise man. Toshiro made it clear what was expected of me at Caltech, but he also really talked to me. He wanted to make sure I understood the materials, the theories and the logic behind what we were doing. That was impressive.

How do you go about finding a mentor? First, start by looking for anyone who inspires you, whether directly or indirectly. It can be someone you read about or see on the news or someone right in your own community. Read current research reports to see who the "hot shots" are in your field. Consider contacting them and asking for a referral to someone you could work with as a mentor. If you ask valid questions about a project you are working on, you will be seen more as a colleague than just a high school student. Attending a meeting of a professional association/science organization can also connect you with people. Contacting local companies and labs is another possibility.

You can find mentors at small state schools, community colleges, volunteer organizations and universities. Look for hobbyists and amateur scientists. Retired people are also excellent potential mentors. Look within your circle of friends and family, your teachers, professors, school administration or community leaders.

A good mentor is someone that will take time to do more than teach you something, but who will show you the why and how behind the lesson. He/she should be willing to answer your questions and explain concepts. It helps if you have similar values and interests as well. Most of all, a good mentor will listen and encourage your "crazy" ideas rather than just tell you why they can't work like other naysayers.

Remember that you can connect with your mentor in a number of ways. You do not necessarily have to see him or her face to face on a regular basis. Your relationship may be based more on emails or phone calls, for instance.

Before you approach someone about mentoring, think about what you are expecting from this person. Do you want connections and networking? Advice? A compassionate ear? A gentle shove when you get bogged down? Know what you need ahead of time.

Check out these online resources for finding a mentor as well:

- www.mentors.ca/findamentor.html

- http://management.about.com/cs/people/a/FindMentor.htm

- www.sciencebuddies.org/mentoring/top_science-fair_mentors.shtml

They often say that behind every successful man there is a loving woman. I would rephrase this to say that behind every successful scientist there is a supportive mentor. Go out and find your Yoda.

Lesson 11

The Power of Research

Y ou might be reading this during your lunch break, working as a summer intern at the National Cancer Institute or you might just be reading this paragraph because it caught your eye as you were browsing through the test prep books. Whether you are an aspiring scientist with research experience already or just an ambitious student aiming to get into a top college, reading this book is a step in the right direction.

First off, you need to know this: there is no RIGHT way to get into research. There isn't any guide you can read that will set you into a science lab in just 12 easy steps. If you look at a group of practicing scientists, you will see that they come from diverse backgrounds. There is no one single experience that will make or break your development.

There are, however, certain steps you can take that will maximize your chances of cracking into the field, getting that foot inside the door. Just like actors move to Hollywood to try to break into show biz and then slowly pick up small time gigs and an agent, there are many approaches you can make in the world of science biz.

Learning to ASK

The key you need to live by from now on is a simple one: You will not know until you ask. Although making assumptions in science can be dangerous, other assumptions can help you achieve goals. I have assumed all my life that I can do something until I'm told otherwise. For example, in high school, I thought it would be exciting to work on cutting-edge cancer research. I had been reading about in magazines and newspapers. I set my sights on the National Cancer Institute and a part of the government's scientific research division, the National Institutes of Health. (I said to aim high, right?)

I really wanted to work there for the summer but I had heard it was almost impossible for a high school teenager to get in. But I had to ask. So I asked all 2,000 or so head researchers at the institute. One afternoon, I sat at the computer patiently cutting and pasting all the email addresses I could find on the NCI site. I nicely stated my desires to find a lab for the summer over and over and over again; and to my surprise, although these were busy researchers with far more important issues to think about (like how to cure cancer, for instance), most responded to me within a couple of days. I ended up being able to pick from several possibilities, not because I was any more qualified than others but because *I asked.*

Learning the Lingo

No matter how much experience you have with research, you need to expose yourself to the language of science. The best way to do this is by reading anything and everything about scientific research that you can find. Keep up with new developments, trends, issues and controversies.

Pick up stories from popular media. These are the stories that usually translate complicated and technical experiments that are fundamentally interesting into something "sexy" and easily understandable for the average Joe. Many of these stories will indicate the hot fields and trends of the time, like research in areas such as stem cells, dark matter or carbon nano-tubes. They will appear in such publications as *The New York Times, The Wall Street Journal, Time, Newsweek* and *US News and World Report.* Some of the most successful young scientists today originally were inspired by reading stories like these and then pursuing them in their own work.

Of course, there are the more technical magazines dedicated to science and new research. They include publications such as *Popular Science, Discover, Scientific American* and *The New Scientist.* These have more in-depth stories on current issues and scientific controversies. They also feature summaries of a variety of exciting new research in everyday language.

Ultimately, the staple of professional scientists is the peer-reviewed research journal. At the end of the day, popular science stories get their information and sources from these journals, where scientists first publish their original research results. Peer-reviewed journals are specifically geared to the scientific community rather than the general public. The papers in them have been, as their titles imply, reviewed by other scientists. While most journalists specialize in a particular niche such as cancer biology or synthetic chemistry, there are still a few publications, such as *Science* and *Nature* that cater to a wider audience.

Taking a Class

Once you have a general background in current science, a good way to dabble in research is to take a class on it. Some high schools offer research classes that teach experimental design and the intricacies of writing a research paper. Many also pair students with a mentor and research lab. Magnet and prep schools in particular frequently list a senior project or research component as a graduation requirement. Community colleges and local universities have many laboratory courses that teach fundamental techniques in conducting experiments in a specific discipline like biology or chemistry. Some even offer a research design class.

Without a doubt, the majority of opportunities to conduct research remain in labs in universities and companies. If you take a college course and get to know some professors, chances are they also run labs that do research. Many professors are very interested in helping teenagers get a foot in the door, especially since having you work in the lab means getting eager (often free) help with their own research.

If you don't know anyone at a university, the best way to find a lab is to browse through the school's websites for the department you are interested in. Here, they will all list the labs in their department and describe the research projects currently going on. Next, send an email to the professor asking if you can help out. The same applies for finding research opportunities within companies; many small companies operate almost like a research institution, with a heavy emphasis on fundamental science.

For many students who know more or less what type of projects they are interested in, going out and finding their own lab works out great. Sometimes the best approach as a teenager, however, is having someone to hold your hand a little bit. I know that I definitely enjoyed not having to worry about every detail of my summer after my junior year when I worked in a bio lab at Caltech. I was accepted to a summer program that provided housing, food and even weekend trips to Hollywood and the San Andreas Mountains. Best of all, I didn't even have to pay for any of it.

Some summer programs also let you take a course in addition to working on a research project. Others may allow you to dabble in several different research fields or just give you a general exposure to the sciences.

There are three main types of research institutions. One is tied to academia and is made up of labs within a university setting. The second is the nonprofit sector, mainly found in the medical field. Several famous cancer centers, for instance, are not affiliated with any particular university but receive the majority of their funding from private donors. They tend to churn out incredible results and research. The last type of research institute is in the private sector. These research institutions range from a race-car designing company run by a cadre of engineers to a chemical conglomerate that has plants on six continents.

Investigating the Trivial

Have you ever been told when constructing an argument that you simply may not compare apples to oranges? Apparently, no one told the researchers at NASA. They took samples from a Granny Smith apple and a Sunkist orange and ground each one into powder and then examined it by a spectrometer. It gave a crude optical fingerprint of objects. They discovered that the apples and oranges are actually quite similar in their infrared spectrum. (So much for that excuse in debates.)

Another research project conducted at a university in Connecticut examined the tragic rise in mortality among senior citizens. Specifically, the research examines the "Dead Grandmother/Exam Syndrome," in which a student's grandmother is far more likely to die suddenly just before an exam than at any other time of the year. Using legitimate sources like the Census Bureau, the professor calculated an almost 20-fold increase in the death rate of grandmothers before an exam. Possible practical solutions he proposed to address this curious epidemic include ceasing giving exams and encouraging more orphans to enroll in college.

Is this legitimate research? Sure. Legitimate research does not mean it won't appear silly or trivial. Although questioning the similarity of two kinds of fruits may seem pointless when there are diseases to be cured, such curiosity to question the ordinary is exactly what may be needed for an unexpected breakthrough. That is why young kids are often the best scientists. They are able to ask uninhibited questions about the world that adults just assume are true or take for granted. The lesson here? If you are considering research, do not be afraid to study the mundane or investigate the trivial.

Following the Scientific Method

So what really qualifies as research and what does not? The two experiments you just read qualify because of two fundamental reasons: the results can be verified and reproduced—not just by the researchers but by a third party—and both studies follow the scientific method.

The scientific method is a rough outline for how new knowledge is acquired through the process of research. Even though school textbooks usually list a series of defined steps, scientists in the real world approach problems in different ways. The bottom line, however, is that research involves making observations and posing a question. Next, you collect enough additional information to form an educated hypothesis (or guess) as to what the answer will be. Then, you design and perform a set of experiments during which you gather and analyze the data. A core component of scientific experiments is to have a control so that you can isolate a single variable and therefore know what to attribute any changes to. Finally, you make conclusions from the results and if applicable, revise your hypothesis and repeat the process.

There are some types of work that are not considered research in the scientific sense. In school, you may have been assigned research papers, book reports or persuasive or informative essays. In the scientific world, these are referred to as *literature reviews*. The research is done in the library rather than the lab. This type of research is secondary because you examine and review someone else's first-hand research. Therefore, it would not be considered original research, i.e. original to *you*.

The stereotypical science fair project of making a baking soda and vinegar volcano is not what I call research. Buying a how-to guide on science fair experiments and replicating one of them is marginally scientific. Research, to me, is the pursuit of original knowledge. This can be done in a high-tech university lab under the supervision of a scientist or in your less-than-glamorous garage. Original discoveries qualify as research.

Many of the Nobel Laureates within the last half decade accomplished things that you will read about in your science textbooks. Not all discoveries are dramatic though. For instance, a high school teenager who competed in the Siemens Competition a few years ago proved the four-color theorem. It states that four colors is all that is needed to color the countries on any map without two neighboring countries sharing a side.

Inventions also count as research. The year I competed in Siemens, the winner developed a power generator that runs on ocean waves. Naturally, science is also about making progress and improvements on existing work.

Appreciating the Perks of Research

At the most fundamental and purest level, research is a pursuit that tremendously challenges your mind. Think of it as the intellectual equivalent to running a marathon but without so much sweating and pain (unless you left the Bunsen burner on . . .). With research, your creativity and ingenuity are challenged in a way that simply is not possible inside a classroom. But the genius of research is that there is no better way to improve your life skills in general. Research teaches you how to manage your time, organize your priorities, write an impressive-sounding paper, talk with confidence and even lose 20 pounds in just two weeks!

Research enables you to truly immerse yourself in a subject. If you are interested in nano-bots or inorganic chemistry, doing a research project in that field will teach you much more than if you read scores of textbooks. Have you ever drifted off in class because the material was too abstract or have you thought some of what you were learning was completely useless in real life? A research experience is the perfect opportunity to apply what you have learned in school—including what you thought of as useless knowledge. If a particular topic intrigues you in class one day, let it be the springboard for further investigation through an independent project.

If you think that research involves spending most of your waking moments toiling away in a basement lab muttering to yourself and eating Cheet-os, think again. Real life scientists spend a fair amount of time publicizing their research results or conducting field experiments, which often means traveling to exotic places. If you want to play around with research but do not want to sacrifice your summer in the Bahamas, now you can do both. Many research areas, especially in ecology and biology, require field work. This can mean anything from trekking the Himalayas looking for invasive plant species to investigating the damages of global warning to reef formations in the Bahamas.

Additionally, internships, summer programs and research competitions are held across the country—and the globe. For instance, I spent one summer in beautiful Pasadena, California (where it is always a balmy 70 degrees) working in a Caltech bio lab through a summer program. I was also able to see the country while competing in science competitions in places like San Diego (including a daytrip to Tijuana, Mexico), Cleveland, Austin and Washington, D.C.

I am passionate about research because it means being exposed to a completely different world than high school or college life. It's a high octane, sexy lifestyle that allows you to go from running experiments in the lab to writing up your research to presenting it to colleagues and the rest of the world.

One part of this unique climate is the people you will meet and the contacts that you make. These may include Nobel Laureates, brilliant professors and industry experts, all valuable later on for help getting your career started or finding a graduate school. Best of all, you will also run into other teenagers who share your excitement, value and interest in research. It certainly didn't hurt my passion for science when I met the discoverer of the *Titanic,* Colin Powell, a panel of Nobel Laureates and the creators of Warcraft.

What if you have absolutely no idea what you want to do after college? Then, besides having a lot in common with me, you will also find doing research a great way to start thinking about finding the perfect career. Working in a lab or spending time tackling a scientific problem on your own are both excellent approaches to see if a career in research is right for you.

Nothing beats real-life experience. Having experience in research while you are still a teenager gives you a huge edge in the pursuit of colleges and careers. When it comes to finding a job or an internship in the sciences, having experience and/or connections with the science world gets your application on a fast track. Even if you decide later on that research is not totally suited to you, the experience might help you narrow down your career choices and it would certainly serve as an impressive indication of your maturity and creativity.

These days, college admission is cutthroat, brutal and stressful. Teenagers are doing everything from helping end poverty in Sub-Sahara Africa to paying thousands of dollars for test prep courses to ensure they get into the college that they want. An overlooked hook that is slowly beginning to catch on is having research experience. To colleges, especially those interested in recruiting additional science students, having research experience is evidence of a focused passion that can accurately predict success in an undergraduate. Plus, research is what most upper-class majors do most of the time already.

Finally, if you have ever had grandiose dreams of leaving a lasting mark and changing the world, start doing research now. There are so many ways that scientific discoveries have influenced everyday life, not just by doubling the life expectancy of Americans, but by allowing us to travel faster, communicate better and live more luxuriously. Your experiment could be published in a scientific journal or you might even be profiled in a national magazine. Your work may be eligible for a patent. And who knows? You might even get a free t-shirt or two. Trust me! They are great when you are too lazy to do laundry in college.

Lesson 12

Do an Independent Project

I grew up in several small, rural towns. All of them had at least one working stoplight downtown. I remember one sleepy place in North Carolina that had a library where I hung out the summer after 7th grade. This town was 70 miles away from the nearest university (Wake Forest). While I do believe that getting started in a research institution is your best bet to really experience how science works, sometimes you have little choice but to start with independent projects because—like me at that time in my life—you are just too far away from other resources.

Independent projects are a good option if you have a brilliant idea you want to pursue. The reality of working in a research lab is that you will be given a project that is within the larger scope of the professor's research interest, which means less room for creativity and individual pursuit. At the same time, if you want to undertake an independent project, there aren't any adults to testify on your behalf when you accidentally unleash a lethal virus . . . or forget to spell-check your reports. The most important key to independent projects is not to be afraid to ask for help. (Sound familiar?) While working on my own projects in the past, I got stuck several times . . . a day. You will too, so finding a patient mentor or someone working on a similar project in the same field will make sure you don't get too lost.

Honey, I'm Home

It is more entertaining to talk about spectacular failures, so I will go ahead and get this story out of the way. One of my first independent projects in high school was a collaborative project with a couple of my good buddies. This, as you will see in just a little bit, is probably NOT a good idea for high school students who get in enough trouble alone as it is.

While aimlessly wandering around the Internet one night, I came across a news article about a bizarre trend in Australia to use honey as a topical antibiotic for burns and sores. This story raised more questions than it answered, which is a good sign that something is a good a project topic. I dug a bit more online and discovered that honey has been used for millennia—all the way back to the Egyptians, as a remedy for countless ailments, ranging from stomach discomfort to eye strain (don't ask; I have no idea!).

Then, I came across a website that sold "medicinal" honey. The stuff was quite expensive—so much so that all these years later I can still remember it was $34.95 plus shipping for an eight-ounce jar. On a whim, I decided to get a jar of the honey, figuring that it was pretty harmless and the worst that could come out of it was to overindulge my sweet tooth. Then, giving a little more thought to the expense involved, I decided to call a few of my friends. I asked them if they would like to work on this project with me, ending each conversation with "and, by the way, could you donate $10 for this miracle honey?"

We received the honey two weeks later. While we were waiting for it, we did some brainstorming. Most of this was not very productive and our sessions were frequently interrupted by long breaks to play Halo. Eventually, however, we came to a consensus on the direction we wanted to go with the experiment. The most basic question to answer was if the honey actually had any antibiotic effects or not. If the results were positive, we wanted to see if it was also effective against antibiotic-resistant strains of bacteria. After all, that was what it claimed on its literature.

Furthermore, we were curious about the exact mechanism by which honey could kill bacteria. Does it work similarly to antibiotics on the market, for example? Would we be able to isolate the active agent in the honey that was responsible for its antibacterial property and then somehow package it as a pill?

It is clear that our project was quickly getting ahead of itself. This is not actually a bad thing as independent projects are perfect for exploring what you are personally curious about and interested in. However, we missed the fact that we really did not have the solid knowledge of biology and experience in the lab to tackle any of this. We decided to enlist the help of an adult and headed off to the local community college to see if we could get some advice—as well as the lab space to do the work.

The first instructor we talked to taught human anatomy. He had neither an idea nor an interest in microbiology. The next instructor we approached pulled out three forms for us to fill out before she would even speak to us. We politely left.

Unbeknownst to us, we left something behind. Let me explain: After receiving our high-priced honey and trying it out ourselves (it was delicious), we had the genius idea of making our own honey. No, we didn't do our research; otherwise, we might have noticed that we needed BEES to make honey. The day before we approached the college, we commandeered my mom's kitchen. We found the biggest pot we could find and poured a five-pound bag of sugar into it. Long story short: we ended up making enough of a crude kind of corn starch to fill several gallon milk jugs.

When we ventured to the college to talk to instructors, we brought some of our homemade honey with us. We figured it demonstrated our initiative and dedication. What we did not realize, however, was that when we left, we had neglected to close the lids on the jugs properly. As we reached the parking lot, we suddenly realized that the jugs were much lighter than when we carried them in. We looked behind us and saw a sticky, splotchy trail of pseudo-honey nicely winding its way from the offices on the third floor.

We spent the rest of the day mopping floors.

Moral of the Story

My first independent project in high school clearly did not go so well. After we were done mopping, our interest in the entire honey experiment fizzled and we decided to move on to more exciting possibilities. But the experience did teach me some lessons that helped with future projects. To save you the same frustrations, here are some points to keep in mind when you are getting started with an independent project:

(1) **The power of one.** Although working in a team means splitting up the work (and cost), many independent projects go much more smoothly if you go it alone. It is also a great opportunity to challenge yourself to handle all aspects of a project, from managing the workload to communicating the results. Collaboration can be a great way to jumpstart ideas or to track down supplies or resources; but often times, when you are working with friends, it is too easy to end up getting distracted. Having said that, I did compete in Siemens with the spam filtering project with a friend of mine.

(2) **Do your research.** Our poor showing at the local college was in large part due to our lack of basic understanding of microbiology and our project goals in general. We knew what questions we wanted to answer, but we really had no idea of how we were going to investigate them. It is vitally important that you read as much as you can about the field your project falls in so that you have a grasp of the problem, but also so that you know what has been done and what is still left to discover.

(3) **Have a game plan.** Do not jump into the project without having an outline of what you will do at each step. We were overwhelmed by naïve enthusiasm at first, which powered us through the first couple of weeks. Without an organized plan, however, we quickly burned out. Having a game plan is a great way for time management, and it also ensures that you will not get to the middle of your project and encounter a

fatal design flaw. A game plan forces you to examine how you will approach a project and if there will be any limitations or constraints to face.

(4) **Find a cheerleader.** A mentor is absolutely critical. It does not have to be a university professor who takes over your project. It could be someone as simple to find as your mom or dad or a high school teacher. The best case scenario is a practicing scientist who is working on similar projects. A mentor should give you advice on the design of your projects and help you troubleshoot any problems that are inevitably going to occur.

(5) **Be ambitious, but stay grounded.** Definitely aim high with any independent project. You will be surprised at how much you know and can accomplish. Our project was ambitious— ultimately, we wanted to develop a pill that has all the medicinal benefits of honey. Sadly, our project suffered from an idyllic naiveté. Make sure you set your sights on something realistic—displacing pharmaceutical companies by coming out with a new miracle honey drug did not fall into this category.

Lesson 13

Publish Your Results

Publishing your scientific results is an important part of becoming a respected scientist. Although each person approaches the writing process a little differently, there are some basic elements you need to include in a paper that you hope will be published. Write them in whatever order feels best to you and works well with the project.

(1) **Your goals and hypothesis.** These should be concrete and clear from the very start. What is your tentative idea to explain your observations, and how do you hope to test it? A hypothesis should make a prediction that can be tested.

(2) **The methods you used.** This is a detailed portion of the paper. Typically it takes up to three to four pages. It should include the specifics of what testing methods were used, what steps were taken and in what order they were done. Describe the experiments you did so that they may eventually be repeated. To make sure the data is accurate and fresh, it is a good idea to keep a journal as you do your project. If you take daily notes, it will help you greatly with your paper. When describing your methods, you have to find the right

balance between providing too much information and not enough. You don't want to be confusing but you don't want to be tedious either. If you have a lot of steps, generalize. If you only have a few, be more detailed. Don't hesitate to more efficiently present something by inserting, "Please see reference X."

(3) **Your results.** This is where you will most likely include graphs, charts, diagrams and other graphics. For tables, don't use more than three or four columns or five to six rows, if possible. Otherwise it looks intimidating and is dull for the reader. Your graphs can be used to show trends, correlations and comparisons. Pie charts are good but stay away from those 3-D ones because they look amateurish. Along with the graphics, be sure to include a paragraph or two that summarizes the material in words. Do not EXPLAIN the hypothesis, just summarize the data.

(4) **Your abstract.** This usually runs about 250 words and acts as a basic overview of the entire project. Emphasize the results and their significance to the world of science. Keep in mind that although this will likely be the first part of your paper that readers see, it is one of the last you do because you cannot complete it until the entire experiment is finished.

(5) **Your introduction.** This is the place where you mention what inspired you to try this experiment, the logic behind it and the overall objectives in simple terms. Did you set out to make a robot? What did you predict would happen? What really did? Was your hypothesis right or wrong (and it's okay for it to be wrong)? Like the methodology section, this should run between three and four pages long.

(6) **The discussion.** This is the section where you talk about why things happened the way they did, relating it all back to your hypothesis, whether you proved or disproved it. How did

everything come together? What limitations are there on the data (i.e. needed more material, samples were not clean and so on)? Were there any shortcomings in the process? If so, what were they?

(7) **The conclusion.** Just like in all of those English class essays you wrote, the conclusion is where everything is tied up. You should focus mainly on pointing out the significance of the results. Don't just repeat everything you said in the other sections.

One of the biggest tips I can give you is to keep a detailed journal from the time you start your project until you are done. It is much easier to remember every step and every factor if you have already written it down.

So, Now What?

Now that you have this brilliant research project all written up, what are you supposed to do with it? More times than not, you will be turning it into a teacher or professor as part of your class grade. There are other options, however, and one of them is seeing if you can get the paper published. Where can you do that? (Not sure what I would have done if you hadn't asked!) Here are some possibilities:

(1) **Enter it into a research competition.** There are district and regional symposiums for this kind of contest. You can also find high school symposiums to enter. Check out the Junior Science and Humanities Symposium at www.jshs.org or the American Junior Academy of Science at www.amjas.org. Here is an example of what the JSHS requires for their research papers (taken from their website):

NATIONAL JSHS - RESEARCH PAPER SUBMISSION

All National JSHS student presenters must submit an electronic version of their research paper for review by the National JSHS judging team. (See www.jshs.org, National symposium section for instructions on electronic submission of the abstract.)

- The paper should be a minimum of 5-6 pages and a maximum of 20 pages, including appendices.

- Photography may not be used in the electronic research paper; photography may be used in the oral presentations.

- Graphs, tables, diagrams, charts or other graphic representation should be simple to allow the judges on-line access to the research paper.

- A maximum size limit for the electronic research paper is 1.8 Mb.

- A recommended outline for the research paper includes:

    1. a title page or cover page stating the student's name, school address and title of the research;

    2. acknowledgement of major assistance received;

    3. table of contents;

    4. if applicable, statement that "research involving non-human vertebrates or human subjects was conducted under the supervision of an experienced teacher or researcher and followed state and federal regulatory guidance applicable to the human and ethical conduct of such research";

    5. introduction;

    6. materials and methods;

    7. results (data or findings);

    8. discussion and conclusions;

    9. references or literature cited;

    10. and appendices (if necessary).

The research paper is used as a supporting document to the abstract during the judging process. The judges read both the abstract and paper.

(2) **Send it to a student research magazine to see if it can be published in a forthcoming issue.** You might try the *Journal of Young Investigators* (www.jyi.org) or look for small student-run high school or college publications that might be interested. For instance, I run a tech magazine mainly for college and grad students which publishes research papers by students in computer science. The magazine, *Crossroads*, is sponsored by the Association for Computing Machinery, and it is the country's largest student technology journal.

Lesson 14

Enter Competitions

How do you feel about receiving a $100,000 scholarship to help pay for college? The Siemens Competition in Science, Math and Technology is just one of dozens of science and research competitions that literally give out millions each year. For instance, I won $50,000 from the Davidson Institute, $25,000 from Discover Card, $10,000 from Toyota and thousands of dollars more from Siemens and Intel.

Why are they so eager to just hand out money? Most of the corporations that sponsor these research competitions are technology or research companies that make a living thanks to the scientists working for them. So it's in their best interest to encourage interest in science among teenagers during a time when the U.S. is threatened by aspiring scientists from abroad and declining science literacy on the home front.

You might think that winning scholarships through science competitions is almost impossible. The truth is that if you have the dedication to complete a research project, you are 90 percent of the way to getting money for college. While millions of teenagers are eligible for various "All-American" or "Top Student" awards, only a relative handful are competing for research scholarships. These types of awards are especially attractive to students who may not be as stellar in other areas of student life. The results of science competitions are usually based on the merits of your project alone and judges are not influenced by outside factors such as whether or not you have a 2400 on your SAT.

Let's take an in-depth look at a few of these competitions:

Siemens Competition in Math, Science and Technology

One of the two most prestigious research competitions alongside Intel— but unlike Intel, Siemens allows teams to compete too and does not consider the individual's other merits

Amount: $1,000 to $100,000

How competitive: 300 semifinalists, <60 regional finalists and 12+ national finalists (referring to projects, since teams of up to three can submit one project)

Application deadline: October 1

More info: www.siemens-foundation.org

Eligibility:

    ✓ Need to be a senior for the individual competition

    ✓ All high-schoolers for team competition

    ✓ U.S. citizenship or green card required

Description

A research competition that is solely judged on the merits of the submitted project, the Siemens Competition is one of the two top science academic awards that a student can achieve in high school. Although the competition only began in 1999, its history stems from the same roots as the Intel Science Talent Search. The original competition was known as the Westinghouse Science Talent Search. When Siemens bought Westinghouse in the 1990s, they lost the sponsorship of the competition to Intel, so they decided to create their own version. Thus, the two competitions are very similar.

However, there are two main differences. First, there is a team option for the Siemens, in which groups of two or three students can work on and compete with the same project. Even better, students don't have to be seniors to compete in the team division, a great option to getting experience in research competitions earlier in high school (which is the path I chose). The second difference is that while Intel wants to recognize the best projects and also the "best scientists," Siemens doesn't consider individual merits. The bottom-line is that if you have a strong project, you'll go far. Otherwise, don't depend on your high SAT scores or teacher recommendations to pull you through.

The competition is split into three stages. In the first stage, 300 semi-finalists are chosen based solely on the research paper. From this stage, up to 60 projects, split between six geographical regions, are chosen as regional finalists. The regional finalists compete amongst each other at various universities such as MIT and Georgia Tech. The individual and team winners from each region go on to compete at the national level, for which the top prize is a $100,000 college scholarship.

Application tips

The application is somewhat lengthy, but definitely not as tedious as filling out the forms for Intel. Your application essentially consists of a 20-page double-spaced report and a mentor evaluation. Instructions about the style and format of the report are specific and detailed, down to exactly how wide the margins should be and which sections you should include. There are no transcripts or personal essays to worry about! Like other research competitions, what's most important at this stage is the quality of your research paper. It should be written in clear, concise English and organized in such a way that judges can follow your logic and conclusions. Also spend time presenting your data in the best way possible for judges to understand your results, whether that is with bar graphs or tables. A crucial point to remember is to successfully convey to what extent your project is your own and how it fits in context with existing work. This could be done in the introduction of the paper and also through your mentor's evaluation.

INSIDER'S LOOK

This is one of the two must-do competitions out there (the other being Intel). Note that Siemens is due a month earlier than Intel. This means that once you have the research report written, you can use it for the other competition. But because of the early deadline, you should try to work on your paper at the end of summer, and have your mentor look over it several times with you to ensure that the science is right. Remember, the judges will all be professional scientists, so it'll be hard to get anything past them.

The 300 semi-finalists are announced on their website. Just to make it that far is a pretty big deal already, but alas, you don't get any money. Shortly after this announcement, but a week before the public announcement for the next stage, you'll get a phone call from someone at College Board (which administers this competition) if you're selected as a regional finalist, which is a *really* big deal. There are up to 60 regional finalist projects in the country. At this point, you'll have to worry about making a fancy poster, preparing a 12-minute PowerPoint presentation and thinking about how you'll handle the special Q&A session with the judges. The regional competitions are held at a research university somewhere in the vicinity. I went to UT-Austin even though I applied from SC (something about not enough teams in the southwest region). It's not really about fun and games since the weekend you're there is pretty intense and basically all about the competition. And by the way, the pre-dinner mixer is *not* optional (the judges come around asking questions about your project).

Intel Science Talent Search

Premier research competition looking for "young Nobel Laureates"

Amount: $1,000 to $100,000 (and free trips)

How competitive: 300 semi-finalists, 40 finalists, 10 national winners

Application deadline: November 15

More info: www.sciserv.org/sts

Eligibility:

✓ High school seniors only

✓ Individual projects only

✓ Excellent grades, recommendations and test scores

Description

This is the oldest research competition for high school students, stretching back to just after World War II. Not only is there scholarship money at stake, but also the prestige and national publicity of winning an Intel prize. High school seniors start by submitting a research paper, along with a very lengthy application that includes several recommendations (one of which is by your mentor). After an additional round of selection, the top 40 finalists are invited to Washington DC for a week of interviews, presentations and even fun (sightseeing and meeting the other participants).

Application tips

If you can make it through this application, you shouldn't have a problem with college applications. The Intel application is probably the most tedious process, next to the Davidson, which requires a videotape! Anyway, for the Intel, you'll have to write several essays, expounding on everything from how your scientific curiosity developed to exactly why your project matters to society. Then you'll have to gather several recommendations, including one from a science/math teacher and another from your research advisor. The selection committee also wants to see your high school transcript and test scores.

Basically, you need to have a very impressive project and be an all-star outside of the lab. They want to see a student who excels in leadership, community service and academics. In particular, you'll want to emphasize how your interests in science all tie together, for instance, if you tutor students in math, founded a math club and also grew up tinkering with model rockets. A few anecdotes about growing up with science (how you romped around in your backyard looking for snails) will help seal the deal.

INSIDER'S LOOK

I never made it to the first round! So please do take my advice with a grain of salt. I thought I spent a good amount of time on my essays—at least a whole day's worth—and also made sure to get decent recommendations, although I didn't really have teachers who knew me outside of the classroom. But I've heard from plenty of students who did make it further in the competition, and here's their advice: Double-check the scientific validity and logic of your paper. Apparently the judges they use are top-notch in their field and look only at papers in their subspecialty. And at the national level, the interview can be traumatic and intimidating. I am told that the judges will ask you crazy questions about philosophy and medical ethics and esoteric puzzles as well as details about your projects that you thought only you would care about.

Intel International Science Fair

The biggest science fair in the world. Period.

Amount: $1,000 to $50,000 (and free trips)

How competitive: Grand Prize in each scientific discipline, along with 1st-4th prizes

Application deadline: competition in early May, regional fairs in spring

More info: www.sciserv.org/isef

Eligibility:
- ✓ High school student
- ✓ Participate in a regional science fair sponsored by Intel

Description

This is the competition that people think of at the first mention of science fairs. Thousands and thousands of high school students participate in one of the regional science fairs. From there, the top students get sent to the international fair, where they compete against students from all over the world. I think standing next to my booth were students from Singapore, China, Russia and Brazil, just to name a few. What's great about this competition is that no matter how serious you are about research, you can still get involved. With competitions like Siemens and Intel, it's hard to make it to the final rounds won't if your project wasn't done in a university lab, but people have done it. But it's possible to win big-time with an independent project—three of the Siemens winners in the last few years worked from home. Ryan Patterson won both Siemens AND Intel STS in 2001 for inventing a sign language translator. Math projects are usually the easiest projects to compete with working out of your home. But with this science fair, the projects that go the farthest are often independent ones that explore an area of science that falls between the cracks in the real world of science.

Application tips

The application process is quite simple: you send in an abstract of your work along with a one page form which has a place for your mentor or advisor (and it can be a science teacher) to sign off on your project. The real work comes during the science fair, when you're expected to give a quick presentation to the judges as they go from booth to booth. You stand in front of your display board to explain your project. The top students (usually two) from each region—my state had three to four, I believe—go on to the international fair, which is held in a big metroplex. The year I went it was held in Cleveland. At the international science fair, the process works the same: you're judged solely on your display board and your presentation (as well as how you answer any questions the judges may have). This is one competition in which you don't need to have a fancy paper in hand, but you do need to be able to discuss your project.

INSIDER'S LOOK

This is a very exciting experience. It's something you can look back on, waxing about those glory days of competing in science fairs. Plus it's a great way of meeting new friends from your area. The local science fair is also an easy way to pick up some scholarship money; I think I landed several hundred the first time I competed. The international science fair is even more of a scholarship cash cow, with hundreds of nonprofit organizations and private companies eager to hand out scholarships and sometimes free trips to top projects. For instance, I received $1,000 from an artificial intelligence association, which was pretty easy to win if you think about the limited number of projects that involve AI. What's also great about this science fair is that you're competing within your own category. If you made a talking robot, you don't need to worry about competing with the bio nerd and his cancer cure two booths down.

Junior Science and Humanities Symposia (JSHS)

A national competition modeled after a scientific conference

Amount: $1,000-$16,000 (and free trips)

How competitive: 250 delegates (5 from each state, 2 of which get to actually compete), 18 national finalists

Application deadline: competition in early May, regional competitions in spring

More info: www.jshs.org

Eligibility:
- ✓ High school student
- ✓ Participate in your state's JSHS

Description

This is a pretty fun competition to enter and relatively under the radar. The great thing is that there's a state competition in almost every state (48 at this point), so you can get involved even if you don't make it to nationals. At the state level, you'll be giving a PowerPoint presentation of your work—for South Carolina, I don't think I even sent in a paper. And if you do, it's secondary to the presentation, which is what counts. The top two participants of the state competition go on to the national symposium to compete for scholarship money. The state fair can elect three other students to go and see what the symposium is all about, but they don't get to compete—a free trip is the consolation prize!

Application tips

Make sure your presentation is well organized and aesthetically pleasing. Don't make amateur mistakes such as trying to have too much text on one page or having the font too small. Also don't speak too fast during the presentation, a common habit when people become nervous. If you're one of the five delegates going to the national symposium, you will need to register on the website within two weeks, and the logistics of how to get there and where to stay will be taken care of by the national organization.

INSIDER'S LOOK

I heard about this competition at the last minute and drove down to the state capital to give my talk. It was all taken care of in an afternoon, and I found out then that I would be one of the two competing in San Diego, where the national symposium was held that year. The symposium was really fun. I got to see San Diego (there was a behind-the-scene tour of the San Diego Zoo, as well as a reception), and we were able to go around to the different talks and meet new friends. I heard relatively early that I wasn't going to make it further in the competition (that's the genius of the selection process), which meant I was able to enjoy San Diego even more. The participants there were all pretty laid back, much more so than at Siemens or Intel.

American Junior Academy of Science

State-wide science fairs that culminate in a national symposium

Amount: $100-$500 (for South Carolina; it differs from state to state)

How competitive: 100 competitors at the state level, roughly 100 at nationals

Application deadline: competitions usually in spring, annual meeting the following February

More info: www.amjas.org or http://astro.physics.sc.edu/NAAS/NAASa.html for state academies

Eligibility:

- ✓ High school student (not necessarily a senior)
- ✓ Some states do not offer the state-level fair
- ✓ Be a member of your state's Junior Academy of Science (for some states)

Description

Depending on how big your state is, with any luck, you'll be able to find a Junior Academy of Science. These are essentially state science academies for high school students that are usually sponsored under the auspice of a State Academy of Science, a professional organization of scientists who get together once in a while to discuss scientific developments, issues and policy. There's also a national version that's basically a who's who of hotshots in science. Each state's academy will sponsor a state science fair in the spring, for which you register by sending in an abstract and a research paper. Of course, the specific rules and regulations differ by states.

The actual science fair is usually not the stand-by-your-poster-while-judges-come-around type you remember from middle school. Rather, they're modeled after symposiums that working scientists hold, in which students give 15-minute PowerPoint presentations of their work in workshops divided by fields (such as biochemistry, physics and medicine). If you do well at the state science fair, you might get the one or two slots (or five in Nebraska) to compete in the national version. These top finishers usually get help to attend the annual meeting for free, or almost free.

Application tips

Getting into the state fair is a piece of cake in many states, but others may be a bit more stringent. Because it's the first level, you already have a good chance of getting prize money or a free trip to the national competition. Just send in an abstract and a paper, and then devote your energy to making an organized and coherent PowerPoint presentation. Practice giving your talk in front of friends who are also interested in science, and see what they think. The practice will also help give you a more polished presentation so that you can convince the judges you know what you're talking about.

INSIDER'S LOOK

Unlike Siemens or Intel, there's no money to win at the American Junior Academy of Science meeting. However, it's a free trip (for most), usually to a big city like DC, where I went, or San Francisco. You are also recognized at a ceremony at the National Academies of Science, a really impressive looking building, and walk across the same stage as the nation's top few scientists. Plus you get a free dinner. The symposium is held at the same time as the American Association for the Advancement of Science (AAAS) meeting, which is a huge event for scientists from all fields. At the 2007 AAAS meeting, I got a chance to hear Google co-founder Larry Page talk about the future of technology. The national event is relatively laid back, involving a poster and oral session. The poster session, when you stand next to your display board and answers question about your research—may be a little more exciting than it sounds, when I attended, Bill Nye the Science Guy decided to drop by! Other than that, you're free to mingle with the other high school participants, attend AAAS sessions and enjoy the exclusive behind-the-scene tours of various science institutions.

Collegiate Inventors Competition

An under-the-radar competition for college inventors

Amount: $15,000-$25,000

How competitive: 15 all-expense paid trips, one $15,000 and $25,000 cash award each, not a very well-known competition

Application deadline: June 1

More info: www.invent.org

Eligibility:

✓ Need to be a college student

✓ Individual or team applications (up to four students)

Description

This is a great competition for students with projects that are more in the realm of products and inventions rather than basic research. The program is designed for students with patentable inventions—you can even submit a patented product, but it can't have been patented more than a year ago. Most of the inventions or products submitted to this competition are in the field of computing, engineering or biotech.

Application tips

The application is fairly straightforward and less tedious than the Siemens or Intel. You are expected to write two essays. One is a 100-word abstract of your project. The other, which can be up to 1,500 words, is meant to explain how your product is new—or how it builds on previous inventions—and also its importance to society. A significant component of the selection process is in evaluating how original your product seems.

You want to explicitly state exactly how your product differs from existing inventions, or really emphasize how it's such an off-the-wall invention that there's nothing like it on the market right now. Another important part of your application is the supplemental material. You're not told what to include, but there are several options: photos, PowerPoint presentation, computer programs or samples of your product (though you're not expected to include an actual prototype of your product). The supplemental material supports what you have written and is essential to giving judges a better idea of your invention.

INSIDER'S LOOK

One quirky loophole to this competition is that you can submit as many entries as you wish. But of course, it's best to focus your energy on one application. A great way of boosting your chances is to get your advisor on your side. It is not required that you develop your product under the supervision of a faculty mentor, but they do want an adult advisor to write a rosy letter championing your invention. If you can get your advisor to say how great the invention is and why it's so unique, that'll definitely be a plus. I never applied for this competition, but there was a similar one sponsored by the National Inventors Hall of Fame, the same organization that runs this competition. I competed in that one, but that died out—probably because it was geared towards high school students and they weren't receiving enough quality applications. But this new version looks like a great venue if you're more of an inventor rather than lab hermit at heart.

Lesson 15

How about Summer Camp?

H ere is an inside look at some of the best science summer opportunities out there. I have done several of these camps and learned a ton—plus met some incredible people. Here is a quick glimpse of what you might try:

Research Science Institute

A summer program sponsored by the Center for Excellence in Education in collaboration with the Massachusetts Institute of Technology

How competitive: VERY! Out of 1,500 or so applicants, only 75 are accepted

Application deadline: all materials are due in February

More info: www.cee.org/rsi/

Eligibility:
- ✓ Completed third year of high school
- ✓ Superior achievement in math, the sciences and verbal arts
- ✓ Potential to become leaders in science
- ✓ Math PSAT score of at least 75 and combined math, verbal and writing PSAT scores of at least 220

Costs: There is no cost for tuition or room and board. The only expense is for transportation to and from MIT.

Description: This six-week program is typically held at MIT. It is a "rigorous academic program" which focuses on "advanced theory and research in mathematics, the sciences and engineering." In addition to working in a lab all day, there are educational discussions at night, often by alums from the program. The lecture series commonly features Nobel Laureates. The college level classes are taught by professors and are designed to sharpen research skills. Students are given the chance to do hands-on research with people at corporations, universities and research organizations.

National Youth Science Camp

This is an intense residential science education program for students during the summer made possible through the National Youth Science Foundation., an organization dedicated to "honor, sustain and encourage youth interest and excellence in science by conducting comprehensive informal science education programs that provide opportunity for constructive interaction with others and emphasize the social value of thoughtful scientific careers."

How competitive: Two delegates are chosen from each state the summer after they graduate from high school. The governor of each state appoints a selection committee who then choose two delegates and two alternates.

Application deadline: decided by the selection committee
More info: www.nysc.org

Eligibility:
- ✓ must have graduated from high school
- ✓ must intend to pursue a profession oriented towards science, math, engineering or medicine
- ✓ shows superior academic proficiency
- ✓ demonstrates leadership abilities and social maturity in school and community activities
- ✓ shows a curiosity and an eagerness to explore different topics

Costs: There are no costs involved at all and even the cost of transportation is included.

Description: This four-week-long summer program (typically late June to early July) is held at a camp near Bartow in the eastern mountains of West Virginia's Potomac Highlands, just down the road from the National Radio Astronomy Observatory at Green Bank. Mornings begin with a lecture from a guest scientist and then students are either taken on an outdoor trip or for a hands-on science seminar. The afternoon is open to a variety of programs including time in the computer lab. Along with science, delegates spend time with normal camp activities like backpacking, rock climbing, caving, kayaking, mountain biking and so on. Near the end, students get to go to Washington, D.C. and tour the buildings plus meet congressmen. There are always surprises involved too.

National Institutes of Health

An eight-week summer training program from the NIH gives students the chance to spend the summer working side by side with some of the leading scientists in the world in an environment that is dedicated to biomedical research.

How competitive: Applicants are chosen by the individual laboratories and branches at the NIH on a rolling basis from November through May. The applications are reviewed and selections are made by scientists in the Institutes and Centers of the NIH. Candidates are told of their selection by the hiring institute.

Application deadline: applications are accepted from November 15 to March 1 and can be done electronically; must include a CV (curriculum vitae), a list of the applicant's publications, a cover letter describing the applicant's research interests and career goals and the names and contact information for two references. Candidates are also asked to specify the specific methodologies or disease/organ systems that interest them.

For more info: www.training.nih.gov/student/sip/info.asp

Eligibility:
- ✓ 16 years or older and currently enrolled at least half time in high school or an accredited U.S. college or university
- ✓ must be a U.S. citizen or permanent resident

Costs: There is a stipend for the applicants who are accepted, based on prior experience. Details can be found on the website.

Description: The program typically begins in May or June and lasts for eight weeks or more. There are opportunities spread out from Bethesda, MD to Baltimore and Frederick, plus Phoenix, AZ, Hamilton, MT and Detroit, MI. There is a lecture series, informal lunchtime talks on training for research careers and a trainee poster day.

NASA Sharp

This NASA summer program is the Summer High School Apprenticeship Research Program. It is geared for students who want an intensive science and engineering apprenticeship program. It begins in mid-June.

How competitive: unknown

Application deadline: applications are turned in by the end of February

For more info: www.dfrc.nasa.gov/Education/Students/Research/sharp.html

Eligibility:
- ✓ U.S. citizen who will be 16 years of age by the time the program starts in June
- ✓ Student with strong interest in and aptitude for a career in mathematics, engineering or the sciences
- ✓ Permanent resident and attend a school within the 50-mile radius of a participating NASA Field Installation, although a residential component is available for those further out
- ✓ Be available every day on a full time basis for the entire eight weeks

Costs: There is a stipend for the applicants who are accepted, based on prior experience. Details can be found on the website.

Description: Activities are kicked off by an orientation. Then students are assigned a Dryden mentor in a specific technical area. Students carry out assignments, prepare written reports and make oral presentations.

Caltech SURF

SURF stands for Summer Undergraduate Research Fellowships. The 10-week long summer program offers weekly seminars by Caltech faculty plus a participatory discussion series on developing a research career.

How competitive: approximately 70 percent of those that apply are accepted

Application deadline: check the website for details

For more info: www.surf.caltech.edu/applicants/index.html

Eligibility:
- ✓ Must be able to devote full effort to conducting the SURF project (you are discouraged to hold a job or take other classes during this program)
- ✓ Must submit progress reports signed by your mentors

✓ Must submit an abstract of your project

✓ Must turn in a written technical report approved by the mentors

✓ Required to give an oral presentation on one of the scheduled seminar day symposia

Costs: SURF Fellows are considered the same as Caltech student employees and are paid $600 per week, which is taxable.

Description: This program offers weekly seminars, a participatory discussions series on career development, social and cultural activities, weekly suppers in local restaurants for small groups of students to have informal conversations with other participants and special field trips.

REU

REU stands for Research Experiences for Undergraduates. It supports active research participation by undergrads in any of the areas of research funded by the National Science Foundation. Instead of an extended camp, the applicant comes up with a potential study idea (either as a team or individually) and applies for funding.

How competitive: unknown

Application deadline: applications are turned in by the middle of August but can differ depending on the program; consult the website for different deadlines

For more info: www.nsf.gov/funding/pgm_summ.jsp?pims_id=5517&from=funl

Eligibility:

✓ You have to submit a proposal for a project to get this funding

✓ The proposed project must be "sufficiently meritorious" and must otherwise comply with the conditions of any applicable proposal-generating document

✓ Applicants must have demonstrated the capability and have access to any necessary facilities to carry out the project

✓ Applicants must agree to fiscal arrangements which, in the opinion of the NSF Division of Grants and Agreements, ensures responsible management of Federal funds

✓ Applicants must be permanent residents of the U.S.

Costs: Usually provided with a stipend and assistance with housing and travel.

Description: NSF funds many research opportunities for undergrads through the REU sites program. This consists of a group of ten or so who work in the research programs of the host institution. Each student is associated with a specific research project, where he/she works closely with the faculty and researchers. Students are responsible for contacting the individual sites for information and application materials. This is all available through REU's online site listed above.

Additional summer programs:

- Cold Spring Harbor Lab
  www.cshl.edu/URP/
- Boston University
  www.bu.edu/summer/program_high_school_students/honors/college_courses/
- Jackson Lab
  www.jax.org/education/ssp.html
- Telluride Association
  www.tellurideassociation.org
- Northwestern University Astro
  www.astro.northwestern.edu/Education/edu_summer_programs.php
- Drexel U Med
  www.drexelmed.edu/GraduateStudies/SummerResearchOpportunities/HighSchoolSummerResearchInternshipProgram/tabid/1077/Default.aspx
- Utah Bioscience
  www.biology.utah.edu/hsprog.php
- MDI Bio Lab
  www.mdibl.org/edu/highschool.shtml
- Gene Almanac
  www.dnalc.org/home.html

Lesson 16

Apply for Scholarships

D o apply. Do NOT procrastinate (see "Senior Year" chapter). Believe me, filling out these applications WILL take much, much, much longer than you anticipate. Start early. Do not wait until the last minute like certain people who shall not be named. If you do, Murphy's Law will come into play and it is almost a certainty that you will run out of paper, your printer will break down or your computer will acquire a virus and eat everything you wrote during the last two hours.

This chapter will give you an insider's look (namely mine) on some of the scholarships that are out there. Please remember that besides the big national scholarships, there are also a number of local opportunities. They may not offer as much money but they also have a lot less competition. You can find information on community scholarships through looking in your school's materials and posted literature, online and by talking to your counselors.

Do not overlook service organizations either. Groups like the Elks, Masons, Kiwanis, Lions and Rotary often have money set aside to help students just like you. Call and ask them if they have any scholarships available and if they do, inquire about the application process. Check with local companies too because they often have money to offer as well.

My basic rule of thumb is that the more time you spend searching for a scholarship, the bigger the payoff is after you find and apply for it.

Another important thing to remember about these scholarship applications is that each one asks for at least one, if not several, *essays*. You will need to sit and brainstorm some ideas for these essays. If you are waiting until the last minute, you will most likely end up going with the tried and true topics like "I won this award once and it changed my life" or "I volunteered for these people and I learned these lessons" or "I suffered through a major tragedy and it made me realize some things about myself." These all sound familiar because they are; almost everyone chooses an essay topic like one of these. You can just imagine how tired essay readers get going over and over the same ideas. You want to create something that no one else could have written.

Start thinking of ideas to write about weeks ahead of time. Find a unique angle to write about. That is how I came up with one of my best essays. You've already read it too—it was the introduction that told you how I chose my name. Pretty sweet, eh?

Here are a few other gems I learned about writing those application essays:

- Never just write about your project because that is not what scholarship committees are looking for. Do not even describe it because it will just make you sound pedantic. Instead, perhaps focus on a problem or an obstacle you encountered while you were doing your project or tell how you became inspired to research the topic.

- Read the prompt and the directions very, very, very carefully and then answer only what is there. This is especially true if you are planning to reuse one of your essays for more than one competition. It's smart to recycle your essays but if you do this, make sure that the essay answers the questions asked.

- Write something that no one else could possibly write other than you. Not sure what that means? Here is a test to find out. It's called the thumb test. Put your thumb over your name at the top of the essay page. Ask yourself if only your name could be there or if any other student's name could be written at the top. Ask a family member, teacher or friend to do the same thing. While other students may be writing about the same topic, think about how you can approach the topic differently.

- Create a spreadsheet with all of the due dates on it, as well as when you should hear back from the scholarship organization. This will help keep you on track.

- Consider doing your applications all at one time so that you only have to ask others for recommendations once or twice instead of repeatedly.

Let's take a look at some of the scholarships I won and see what each one requires.

Davidson Fellows Scholarship

A rather open-ended and hefty scholarship for science and tech projects (humanities subjects as well) that is not as popular as other grants, but definitely worth applying for.

Amount: $10,000, $25,000 or $50,000

How competitive: Around 10 awarded annually

Application deadline: preliminary application due mid-March, entire application due at the end of March

More info: www.davidsonfellows.org

Eligibility:
- ✓ You need to be under 18 years old when you apply (see website for exact age requirement)
- ✓ No minimum age requirement
- ✓ U.S. citizenship or permanent residency
- ✓ Must attend the awards ceremony held in September in D.C.

Description

This scholarship is more like the Siemens and Intel competitions, in that while it's a scholarship, it comes down to the merits of a particular project, more so than the merits of your academic or extracurricular achievements. It's funded by a foundation that was started in 2001 by Bob and Jan Davidson, an extremely nice couple who made a fortune during the tech boom (including owning Blizzard Entertainment, which made Warcraft and Starcraft) and are now in the business of philanthropy.

The scholarships are awarded based on how significant the project is and its potential to benefit society. They don't really show a preference for applied or theoretical projects—in the same year, you might see scholarships awarded for a novel gadget and a math theorem. The categories that are eligible include science, mathematics and technology. A new category called "outside the box" has also been created, which is for university graduate-level work (or the equivalent) that was conducted under the guidance of a supervisor or mentor.

Projects are judged by professionals who work in a related field. The selection criteria include the following: the quality and scope of the entry (worth half), the significance of the work (30 percent) and your understanding of the project and the field. The best projects are awarded the top prize, being named a Davidson Fellow Laureate and given a $50,000 college scholarship. Davidson Fellows are awarded $25,000 and $10,000.

Application tips

Do not be intimidated by this application process. This is one of the most time-intensive applications and may seem like too much of a burden. But the up side is that if you have the dedication to complete this application, you'll have all the materials needed for other scholarships or competitions. Also, I have a feeling because of the high demands of the application, not as many people apply for this scholarship compared to other competitions such as Siemens or Intel STS.

One of the earliest requirements you'll need to think about is having three reference letters. One must come from a mentor or supervisor of the project, another from a teacher and the third from a professional in the field of the project. Another wieldy requirement is a 15-minute video that shows you explaining your project and its significance. Once you've turned in your preliminary application—don't worry, this is only a page with a short essay that tells about your project—you should start working on the actual application.

The application is different for science, math and tech projects. It involves writing a formal research report (with no page limit) and preparing a computer or physical model. This can be an actual computer program if you have a tech project or something as straightforward as a PowerPoint presentation if you have a biomedical project. Finally, you need to write three rather lengthy essays about your work.

INSIDER'S LOOK

The rewards are definitely worth the time and effort of applying for this scholarship. If you have a "prodigious" project—for example, if you spent a couple summers in a university lab or if you've invented a gadget—then you have a great shot at winning big. I had no idea that my project was going to get me anywhere, but I ended up being named a Davidson Fellow Laureate and winning $50,000, the top prize. The Davidson scholarships also have the least restrictions of any that I've won; you can use it for science research and also study abroad.

To maximize your chances, make sure you have very enthusiastic references. I know for a fact that my references were called by the Fellows program when I was on the short-list for the top prizes. Apparently the questions they asked them were pretty much what was already said in the letters. Also make sure that your video shows off your knowledge of the project and field; you want to convince the judges that you know everything there is to know about your project. It's also good to come off as articulate and confident. One of the judges said that a big factor in my winning entry was the strength of my video. I had practiced it until I didn't need notes.

Perhaps one of the biggest rewards of the scholarship is the connections you'll make. The awards ceremony in D.C. was a great opportunity to meet the other Fellows, some of whom won their scholarships for talents in music and the humanities. For instance, one girl who won in my year has been composing internationally-acclaimed symphonies for years.

You also get to personally know the Davidsons, who are really a genuinely nice couple. Jan Davidson actually donated $1,000 to my fundraising campaign for Habitat for Humanity.

The foundation makes an effort to have scholarship recipients meet important leaders while they are in D.C. I met my congressman and sat in on a meeting with an Assistant Secretary of Education.

Discover Card Tribute Award

A relatively less competitive scholarship for juniors who show academic and community achievements, as well as having overcome a roadblock.

Amount: $2,500 for state winners, $25,000 for national winners

How competitive: 300 state winners, 10 national winners

Application deadline: January 31

More info: www.discoverfinancial.com/data/philanthropy

Eligibility:
- ✓ High school juniors only
- ✓ Need a 2.75 cumulative GPA in the 9th and 10th grade
- ✓ Accomplished in leadership and community service, along with overcoming a "significant roadblock or challenge"

Description

When a scholarship is sponsored by a credit card company, you know they're going to be generous. This scholarship stands out because it's only for juniors, which makes it slightly less competitive because you're not competing against all high-schoolers in the country. Once you send in your application, there are two rounds of judging. State winners are first determined, with states that have more applicants usually getting more state winners. The top state winners are then automatically considered for one of up-to-10 national awards. If you live in a small state, definitely apply because each state always has at least a couple of winners.

Application tips

When I won one of the $25,000 national awards, a third of the awards were reserved for applicants with talents in science. For me, this meant emphasizing my spam filtering project and achievements at science fairs. But it seems now the scholarship is focusing much more on leadership and community service with no reserved slots for science applicants. That doesn't mean you shouldn't apply, but just make sure you relate your science background to leadership and community service experiences. For instance, I talked about volunteering at the local hospital because of my interests in biomedical research and also how I enjoyed tutoring other students in science and math courses.

The scholarship program is now administered by a company that specializes in managing scholarships, so the application is rather straightforward and is completed online. Because this application doesn't require a lot of material, make sure you make each word count. For the essays, tie everything back to community service and leadership. And perhaps what will make or break your application is your experience in overcoming a "significant roadblock or challenge." I talked about having to go to five different schools in six years and also having to deal with an emergency intestinal surgery.

INSIDER'S LOOK

The key to winning this scholarship is quantity. Yes, quality is very important, but unlike the Davidson scholarship for instance, you don't want to focus on just a single project. My approach with Discover Card was to list all the extracurricular activities that I was involved in and then made sure that I spelled it out word for word how they related to community service, leadership or science (the three criteria that were in place when I applied).

Back then, the scholarship was administered in-house, which meant that it was much more personal. Nowadays, because it's run by a scholarship company, you'd want to be much more "keyword" and results oriented, making sure your application will make it past a quick glance by some program administrator.

The new policies on the scholarships are rather restrictive; the checks are sent off directly to the school and are divided over four years. But if you're lucky enough to be a national winner, you'll have a great time. They fly you out to Chicago where you visit the Discover Card headquarters, and they put together a glitzy awards ceremony attended by a thousand employees. It's a very glitzy event—when we walked onto the company campus that day, there was a huge banner with pictures of the national winners draped across the entrance.

Tylenol Scholarship

A rather obscure scholarship for students who will major in a health-related field in college.

Amount: $1,000 and $5,000
How competitive: 150 for the $1,000 and 20 for the $5,000
Application deadline: September 30
More info: http://scholarship.tylenol.com
Eligibility:
   ✓ High school senior
   ✓ Will major in a health-related field

Description

Not much is really known about this scholarship beyond the brief one page explanation on Tylenol's website. The scholarship is also not well advertised, so you should give it a try—especially since they give out 150 $1,000 awards. The scholarships are for high school seniors who want to major in a health-related field in college. You will be judged on your academic and leadership abilities, so grades are very important as well as your extracurricular activities (and the leadership positions that you hold in these groups).

Application tips

Because this scholarship is administered by the same company that runs the Discover Card program, the application is pretty straightforward. It also means you don't have to send a recommendation letter. The essays are short (500 and 100 words), and I believe the selection process mainly comes down to looking at your grades and a list of extracurricular and leadership achievements. I can't really tell you exactly how to win, since I didn't. The selection seemed somewhat arbitrary, but then again, I didn't spend much time on my application at all.

USA Today All-USA Academic Teams

A very prestigious scholarship that's more about the honor than the money, for all-around good students who have a single big project.

Amount: $2,500 personal check

How competitive: 20 nationally on "first team," 40 on the second and third teams and more honorable mentions, but with no money attached

Application deadline: February 20

More info: http://allstars.usatoday.com

Eligibility:

- ✓ For the high school team, high school senior or junior who is graduating early
- ✓ Have a single "intellectual endeavor" to discuss

Description

This is a cool scholarship, not because you're going to get a lot of money out of it (although the money comes in the form of a personal check, which is very nice), but because of the publicity and prestige attached to the award. The 20 students on the "first team" are featured on a two-page spread and mentioned on the front of the "Life" section of an issue of the paper some time in May. The downside is that they don't fly you out to a snazzy rewards reception or weekend getaway so you'll meet the other winners—you'll have to make do with their profiles.

The scholarships are usually given to all-around awesome students, although the biggest factor is your "hook." This means that you'll need to bring to the table your most impressive "intellectual endeavor," which will likely be your research project. If you take a look at the profiles of past winners, you'll see that most go off to the Ivy League or other top schools. They each have top grades, leadership positions in extracurricular activities and a list of other scholarships won.

Application tips

Similar to the Davidson scholarship, this one requires three separate references. One is a nominating reference which should talk about your particular project, while the two others can be from pretty much anyone. You'll also need to get your principal to sign off on your nomination, although (don't worry!) there can be more than one applicant from each school.

The single most important part of the application is the 500-word essay on your project. This essay will need to be like an extended abstract of your work, with an intro, brief methods and results. But don't fall into the trap of making it too technical, just include enough that the judges will be confident that you know what you're talking about. Make sure to leave room to talk about the significance of the project and how it will improve society. The judges will be looking at the originality of the project, the results and its impact on society. Beyond this essay, make sure your course load, grades, extracurriculars, awards and summer activities are top-notch.

INSIDER'S LOOK

Beyond Siemens and the two Intel programs, this scholarship probably gets the most coverage. I definitely felt an extra surge of pride for winning this award; it's not every day that your profile and picture appear in a two-page spread within the paper. They actually sent over a photographer to shoot countless headshots and poses, and on top of that, I got to miss a class for the photo shoot!

In general, if you're going to do well in Siemens and Intel, then you'll do well with this scholarship. In fact, they like to make a point of saying which other scholarships a winning applicant has won (such as Siemens and Intel). Don't get discouraged about applying if you don't think that your project is necessarily up to par. Being an all-around good student will make up for a project that's somewhat lacking. In other words, because they're not judging your project as a scientific paper, it seems you just need to wow them on the concept—and your grades! And don't fret if you don't make the first team; there are still at least 40 slots left that will still make a huge difference to you during college admissions. But alas, they don't come with a personal check.

National Merit Scholarship

One of the largest academic scholarship programs out there, with lots of money handed out for being an all-around good student (and a good test-taker!)

Amount: $2,500 unrestricted scholarships, upwards of $10,000 if it's college or corporate sponsored

How competitive: ~2,500 of the unrestricted scholarships, thousands of the college and corporate sponsored scholarships

Application deadline: February for finalists; take the PSAT in junior year to be initially considered

More info: www.nationalmerit.org

Eligibility:
- ✓ Take the PSAT as a high school junior
- ✓ U.S. citizen or green card holder

Description

Sponsored by a nonprofit whose main mission is running this program, the National Merit scholarships are famous for the "brand," not necessarily the money they give out. Considering that almost all high school students "enter" the scholarship process by simply taking the PSAT, it's somewhat hard to get one of the actual scholarships. But if you work it right, you might be able to get a hefty scholarship from a particular college, especially if it's a state school looking to attract top students away from the Ivy League. Some of these schools can cut off $10,000 from your bill just for being a Finalist.

Scholarships are also handed out by corporations who partner with National Merit to award deserving students. These are usually given to the children of employees (so if your parents work for one of the corporations that participates, let the National Merit program know that).

Out of the 1.5 million students that take the PSAT as juniors, about 16,000 semi-finalists are named. These are calculated by state and are based on the test scores. Each state has a quota of semi-finalists based on population. Some very big states, such as California and New York, have very high cutoffs such as 220, while other states (like mine) had lower cutoffs, for example, around 205. Most of the semi-finalists make it as finalists, at which point you actually have to fill out an application to receive any sort of money.

Application tips

Around 15,000 Finalists are given applications for a merit scholarship. Half of the finalists receive some sort of scholarship offer, although only roughly 2,500 receive the most coveted "unrestricted" scholarship. On the application, make sure that you check the list of colleges that offer merit scholarships, and choose the one that you would most want to receive a scholarship from. Your first choice college is given the option of awarding you a renewable scholarship. This may turn out to be much more lucrative than the $2,500 unrestricted scholarship, although the caveat is that you would have to go to that particular college.

The application is pretty straightforward; it asks for a reference and one 500-word essay. Because you have a science background, you can paint a unified and coherent picture of you as a solid student who stands out because of your research efforts or interest in science. Don't focus on a particular research project too much, but also don't make your application so bland that it blends in with the thousands of other applications.

INSIDER'S LOOK

For me, this was one of the easier scholarships to try for because you really don't have to do much until you receive the application for finalists. Just make sure that you sign up for the PSAT as a junior, as that's the only way to be eligible for the program (you could theoretically still participate if you have a really good reason for missing the PSAT).

The application is also pretty easy to fill out. If you're from a small state, chances should be good that you'll get at least some money out of the program. If you're from a big state, it might be harder because there are many qualified students (and the money is handed out on a per-state basis).

Robert C. Byrd Honors Scholarship

A federally funded program that gives out a huge chunk of money to all-around decent students, so definitely don't miss this opportunity

Amount: averages $1,500 per year for up to four years

How competitive: 27,000 nationally; each state has a quota that varies by population

Application deadline: varies by state

More info: www.ed.gov/programs/iduesbyrd/index.html

Eligibility:
- ✓ High school senior
- ✓ U.S citizenship or green card holder

Description

This is an often overlooked gold mine for help funding your college bills. The government has allocated enough money to essentially pay $6,000 over four years to 27,000 students. And this happens each year! Keep in mind that although it's funded by Congress, the scholarship is state-run. That means each state has its own quirks and rules and deadlines. In general, you'll want to be a good student with top grades, a rigorous course load and impressive test scores. Beyond that, you should be able to use your science background and project to get you noticed above the other applicants.

Application

The application process differs by state. For my state, South Carolina, there was a pretty brief form that required a teacher's recommendation as well as transcript and a list of my activities. But other states, such as New York, have so many awards to give out that they simply use a formula to determine the winners. In that case, applicants are ranked by county based on a combination of GPA (75 percent) and SAT score (25 percent).

Looking at the application process for a few states, it seems the bigger states use a more quantitative approach to selecting the winners, which might be perfect for you if you have top grades and SAT scores. In those cases, a 3.9 GPA and 2100+ SAT score is expected, although you might need to do even better in competitive states. For less populous states, the application process is more like for a generic scholarship. For Colorado's selection process, you need to provide a reference letter, write an essay and send in your transcript. But even for this amount of work, the potential payoff is still pretty appealing.

INSIDER'S LOOK

Although the federal government stipulates that every high school must be notified of this opportunity, it usually flies under the radar. This means that your chances for winning one of the grants are even higher if you just remember to apply! Make sure you don't miss the deadline, which differs by state. Since it is run by the state government, the guidelines and applications are sometimes not readily available. Some states have the applications only available through your guidance counselors while other states actually have an online application.

Once you send off the application, prepare to wait for a few months with little word. I believe I emailed the state administrator several times asking for any news. She must've gotten quite annoyed and probably gave me the award just to shut me up. If you do win one of the awards, make sure you renew it each year (yes, if you forget to renew, you'll lose the scholarship).

Timely Tips for College

Much of the information in this section of the book will sound somewhat familiar to you. No, it's not déjà vu or telepathy. I talked about much of this in earlier chapters. I have tailored them in this section, however, to be very specific tips to help you with whatever college you choose.

Tip 1

Highlight Your Projects

This section is about how to take the project(s) you have done and make them work to your advantage. Colleges and scholarship committees truly value extracurricular activities as we have already talked about because they want to see that you do more than just show up for class. Projects are especially valuable because they clearly show that you know how to work independently, how to define a research question and how to conduct research. Projects also demonstrate tangible end results such as a project or paper being published. It is truly important that you explain not just what you did but why you did it, what you accomplished and what you learned from the whole experience.

- If either your scholarship or college admission forms require a short response or an essay, write it about your lab experience. Talk about what you learned—but don't bore this non-science reader with every little detail. Include an anecdote that reveals how you were able to overcome an obstacle or something similar.

- Make it clear how much of a time commitment this project took. For example, did you spend 40 hours a week for 12 weeks over the summer? Was it three hours a day after school? Reporting this shows that you are able to stay committed and that you are responsible.

- Take advantage of any research opportunities that open up, such as competitions, scholarships and summer internships.

- Stick to one or two projects and follow them through to the end. Don't abandon them like a certain someone did with a honey project ...

- See if you can get published. Be sure to read the chapter about this first though.

- Participate in a science fairs.

- Apply for some research scholarships.

Tip 2

Get Recommendations

In this section, we will take a look at how important having solid recommendations or referrals are to your years in college and beyond. Colleges want to know not only what you think of yourself (heck, you're just a tad biased) but what others think about you also. Most colleges and scholarship organizations ask for recommendations from teachers, counselors and others who know you well. Here is how to make sure you get some of the best possible references:

- Be on good terms with at least one teacher in the sciences and one in the humanities.

- Find a teacher who knows you outside of class, especially an advisor to a club. Let the teacher learn who you are as a person instead of just another student.

- It is powerful to have people like your teachers and counselors on your side, so use this wisely.

- Ask your research advisor for a recommendation and have him emphasize character traits like independence and the ability to problem solve.

- Ask the person to de-emphasize the adjectives (good, smart, quick, bright, etc.) and emphasize the verbs (led, held, organized, performed, etc.)

- Ask the people recommending you to compare you with other students, i.e. "He is one of the most organized students I have ever known" or "She is the most dependable student I've had in my classes."

- Ask the person to provide meaningful anecdotes in the recommendation. These should be stories that demonstrate your best traits as well as show that the person knows you well.

- Ask for recommendations early. Give the person at least a full week to complete it. You want to get your request in before the onslaught of other students begins. You do not want your recommendation to be halfway down a huge pile—you want it to be the only one on the desk.

- Provide a resume or a list of your accomplishments to help the person remember your achievements. Also give a cover letter that explains what the letter will be used for, what the college or scholarship organization wants information about and when the deadlines are.

- Remember that a recommendation is typically a letter but it might also be a phone call to the right person.

- If you need letters for both college admissions and research competitions, ask the person to write two separate letters so they can be specifically tailored to the goal. Most likely you will use these letters repeatedly so you want them to be just what you need.

- If you haven't heard back from the person writing the recommendation letters, don't be afraid to give him/her a quick reminder. It doesn't happen often, but references, even with the best intentions, have at times forgotten to write a letter.

Tip 3

Make the Most of Scholarships (and More!)

This section looks at applying for scholarships and then making the most of them once you get one. Science scholarships, oddly enough, are some of the most overlooked types. Students often gloss over any applications that require more than an application form and essay. This is YOUR opportunity to take advantage of other students' laziness.

- The busiest time to apply for scholarships will be during your senior year. Many have deadlines in the fall and spring. While it is a lot to balance both scholarship and college applications in the fall of your senior year, you do not want to miss any opportunities.

- Apply for as many scholarships as you can. Do not limit yourself.

- Remember that scholarships and grants are great, but they will affect the financial aid packages that you are eligible for. Still, it is better to receive a scholarship or grant that you do not have to pay back even if it means that you will receive less in student loans.

- Apply for local scholarships—find the ones that others tend to overlook.

- Find some scholarships while are you are still in your freshmen and sophomore year. Some of them let you apply as early as 13 years old!

- Allot enough time for the scholarship process. The first one will most likely take you three to four hours or more. It takes a while to write a good essay, plus you have to organize a lot of diverse and scattered information. Once you have done it, however, it will cut time off the subsequent ones since all the information is gathered and ready to go.

Tip 4

Consider the Tech Schools

Sometimes when you are searching for colleges, you can overlook some of the best choices. It's easy to do because there are a great many schools out there and the information is massive and overwhelming. This tip focuses on one of those sometimes missed type of schools— the tech schools. See what they have to offer.

- There are some great engineering state schools.

- Tech schools tend to offer less expensive tuition, a solid education and great opportunities for research. Some perennial favorites include North Carolina State, Georgia Tech and Virginia Tech.

- Consider private schools as well. Some brand name places with world labs and professors include Caltech, MIT, Carnegie Mellon and Rensselaer Polytechnic.

- These schools are really ideal for people who know they are primarily interested in engineering or the sciences. They are less ideal for those who might also be just as interested in the humanities or the social sciences.

- These schools have a very competitive campus atmosphere.

- They have a wonderfully "quirky" student population.

- The smaller tech schools often have more openings for those who want to work in a lab.

Tip 5

Hone Your Hook

You know you're special. Your parents agree. Your grandparents definitely agree. Most likely, your friends will even chime in on your behalf. BUT when who you are comes down to just what you can put on paper and you are one of thousands, it's hard to appear special. That is why "honing your hook" is so essential. This makes you stand out from the crowd as someone who is memorable and grabs the attention of the people you need to sit up and take notice.

- You have to do something to make yourself stand out among a pile of 20,000 other great student applications.

- Present yourself as an oddball type—I was a "research nerd" in my applications. Maybe you are a Violin Virtuoso, Chemistry Guru, Gadget Guy, Rocket Man or Computer Whiz. Create a catchphrase that admissions officers will remember.

- Tailor your outside interests into a coherent story, i.e. if you harbor a passion for biology, do research in a bio lab, take a summer bio field class or participate in the Bio Olympiad, then turn that into a story you can tell.

- Colleges are looking for a well rounded class, not necessarily a well rounded student.

- As covered in an earlier chapter, you want to have good grades but also participate in other activities like community service, clubs and organizations.

- Start early but remember that you do not have to be able to figure out your passion tomorrow.

- Do not try to do too much. Branch out and explore but gradually begin to focus on one or two major areas.

Tip 6

Covering Your ... Bases

This tip is all about how it is fine to be great in science, but that should not be the end of who you are or what you learn. Take time to go beyond the science programs you usually study. For example, I did computer stuff and also worked as a tutor for other students. What kinds of things can you do?

- **Community service** is a great idea. You can learn unexpected skills and meet some wonderful people who might just prove to be the connections you need somewhere down the road. It is also a way to give time and energy to a community that you might be turning to eventually for scholarships, references or more.

- Consider learning how to play a **musical instrument** or joining a **choir.** Music has a lot to do with creativity, math and even science—plus it is fun. I believe I learned many things from my years of playing violin. I started at three years old and played until I was about 17. I felt it expanded my mind quite a bit and actually "hard-wired" it in ways that helped me in a variety of subjects later on.

- Learn how to **play a sport.** I played tennis and basketball in high school and now that I am at Yale, I joined the rowing club. Physical activity can help you de-stress and keep you energized. It also gives you time to think. I often worked out scientific problems while I was jogging or hiking.

- Join a club. Take a class in leadership. Become the editor of a publication. Each one of these activities makes you a more well-rounded person. They feed into a coherent package of who you are and who you will turn around and represent to admissions officers.

If you are not sure why you need to develop other aspects of your education, look at it this way. You cannot cruise into some of the best colleges in the country just on good grades, even if they are straight A's. That simply is not enough. There are a lot of students out there with a 4.0 GPA. You have to have more than that to show off when you approach colleges. They are not looking for just the brightest students who knew what they had to do to get good grades. They want the student who has developed him- or herself the most—and that is where all these other types of education come into play.

I look at the other students I know here at Yale. They are good examples. Of course, they have great grades, but there is more to them than that. One guy I know speaks more than a dozen languages. A girl I met already has several patents in place for things she has invented.

Remember that a high GPA or a high class rank or a perfect standardized test score is not enough. Your SAT scores don't have to be perfect either—everything just has to be high enough to be competitive and from there, you support it all with the other activities I just told you about. They show that you are not only bright—you are truly exceptional.

Tip 7

Work at a University

This should sound quite familiar because we have talked about my experiences working at universities earlier. Here are some of the best tips on how to get into one and use what you learn there to further your career.

- Email is the best way to contact professors. Feel free to follow up after a week since many are busy with classes and/or traveling.

- Contact professors early in the second semester to try to get a gig for the summer, or during the summer if you want to start working during the school year.

- Do not be afraid to contact multiple professors at once and see what kind of response you get.

- Use networking. If a professor does not have room in his/her lab, ask if he/she knows of someone who might.

- Do not set your expectations too high. You will have to pay your dues and see how the lab dynamics go.

- Ask for more responsibilities and hopefully your own project or at least a project where you have a great deal of independence rather than just doing someone else's grunt work.

- Keep a notebook and be organized. Write down every instruction so you will not have to ask more than once or forget a step.

- If there are no big research universities, try a smaller liberal arts college or community college. You can also look in the private sector.

Tip 8

Create a Resume

When it comes to writing a resume, the first thing is to determine who the resume is for or what its goal is. Are you applying to a college to get in or are you applying to a company for a job? That will change what type of information you include and highlight.

Let's start with one of the biggest mistakes that everyone tends to make when putting together a resume: overdoing it. A resume is not an excuse to jam every little detail about your life onto a piece of paper. Too much information is not usually a good thing. You do not want to overwhelm the person reading your resume; you want to impress him/her. The main way to do this is to know what to highlight. I found this out when I sent in my application to Yale to see if they would take me. I had put the process off for forever and was down to the wire to get it in. (I honestly did not want to go to Yale at the time, so it was not a high priority for me.) When I finally got around to it, I put together the bare minimum of information—far less than what I usually sent. I didn't even send in a one-page resume, which I did for other schools. I figured I had blown it. Instead I got a pre-acceptance letter from Yale— something that only about 100 of the 20,000+ applicants ever see.

So, what should you include?

(1) **Focus on the extracurricular activities you did.** Don't outline each class and each grade you got—the people reading your resume have already seen this a million times. Instead show what you did after school, on the weekends and in your free time. Remember those bases we mentioned covering before? This is where that information will come in mighty handy.

(2) **Explain any of your research and lab experience.** Tell about your project but remember to phrase it in interesting terms and not scientific jargon. Mention what lab techniques you have learned, what equipment you learned how to use, etc.

(3) **Mention your awards but don't dwell on them or put them at the top.** That makes you look conceited and full of yourself. You can put them in the order of importance or chronological order, whichever you prefer.

(4) **Outline some of your most interesting jobs.** Talk about your responsibilities, how many hours you put in, what kinds of skills you learned—and of course, how all of this contributed to your development and maturity.

(5) **If you have any exceptional abilities, now is the time to add them.** Do you speak multiple languages? Do you know high tech computer skills? Do you invent gadgets in your spare time? Have you built a rocket in your backyard? Talk about it.

(6) **If you are applying for a job, you might also want to include extended contact information like your social security number.**

To see how I put together one of my resumes, look below.

Jerry Guo
Yale University
jerry.guo@yale.edu
345 Temple St.
New Haven, CT 06520

EDUCATION

Yale University, New Haven, CT
   B.A. Economics, expected May 2009
Riverside High School, Greer, SC
   Class rank: 1 out of 333, GPA: 4.0
   SAT I: 800 Math, 800 Verbal, SAT II: 800 Writing, 800 Chemistry,
   800 Biology

EXPERIENCE

Science, Asia News Bureau (Summer 2006–Present)
   Freelancer: Write features on China, including an investigative piece on
   the gene therapy industry, science curriculum, river dolphins and pandas;
   another piece from Galapagos

The Scientist, Philadelphia, PA (2007–Present)
   Freelancer: Written two pieces on pandas and China's "Green Wall"

ACM Crossroads, New York, NY (2003–Present)
   Editor-in-Chief: In charge of the country's most popular student
   computing journal, with 20,000 print subscribers. Budget of $100,000,
   advertisers include Microsoft and NSA

Yale Evolutionary Biology Lab, New Haven, CT (Summer 2006–Present)
   Researcher: Traveled to the Galapagos Islands under a *National Geographic*
   project to study giant tortoises, analyzing genetic samples now

National Cancer Institute, NIH, Washington D.C. (Summer 2005)
   Researcher: Sequenced genes involved in advanced-stage breast cancer

California Institute of Technology, Pasadena, CA (Summer 2004)
   Researcher: Conducted lab work in developmental plant biology

ACTIVITIES

Yale Daily News, New Haven, CT (2005–Present)
Staff Reporter: Yale Law School beat, broke story on future of Yale organic dining, gender inequities at the architecture school (arts & administration beat last year)

Science Whiz: How One Student Used Science to Get into College and Win $100,000 in Scholarships, SuperCollege LLC (to be published Fall 2007)
Author: Writing a full-length book about conducting scientific research in high school

Yale Journal of Medicine and Law, New Haven, CT (2005–2006)
Associate Editor. Edited and wrote stories

Yale Heavyweight Crew Team, New Haven, CT (2005–2006)
Freshman Rower

AWARDS

Davidson Fellow Laureate, $50,000 national scholarship for research (2004)

Discover Card National Tribute Award, $27,000 scholarship for science/tech (2004)

USA Today All-USA Academic Teams, awarded to top 20 U.S. students (2005)

Toyota Community Scholar, $10,000 national scholarship for volunteerism (2005)

Siemens, Regional-Finalist, a national research competition (2003)

SKILLS

Computer: Excel, PowerPoint, Java, VB, C++, HTML
Language: Mandarin (fluent), Spanish (beginner)

Tip 9

Enjoy the Summer after Graduation

This tip will be short and sweet because my message here is simple: make the very most of your summer after high school and before college. This is one of your last chances to explore what you want to do with your life, to understand what you like the most and to pinpoint in what directions you want to go—and not go.

So, what do you do with these three special months?

(1) **TRAVEL.** If you can go there, do it. If you have the money, pay it. If you don't, earn it. The world is out there waiting for you so don't let it pass you by. Grab any opportunity you can to see it.

(2) **DO LAB RESEARCH.** Find a lab to work in and learn. The experience is invaluable. It looks mighty great on the resume.

(3) **TAKE SUMMER CLASSES.** If at all possible, take these classes in a different geographical area. Try for another country. If not, try for the opposite side of the country.

(4) **ENROLL IN A SUMMER SCIENCE PROGRAM.** Go to a camp or some kind of official science program. I went to the National Youth Science Camp when I was 17. We were allowed to dissect a human hand—it was awesome, very complex and graphic.

This special summer is your last chance to take a breather before the education for your career begins. Please, make the most of it. Learn about yourself and have fun!

Conclusion

A long time ago, when I was just a little kid watching "Tom and Jerry" cartoons, I don't think I could have ever envisioned that I would one day win scholarships and be going to Yale on what I had earned. It has been a wonderful trip so far and I know that I have countless scientific experiences still waiting for me. Science is a living organism that is always changing from day to day. I'm very lucky to be a part of this world and love waking up each day and learning something new. I hope to continue exploring the farthest corners of the world with leading scientists in their fields and come back to write about it. Most of all, I know that being a "science nerd" is one of the best things I have ever done with my life and I hope you make the same decision I did. The world needs more nerds like us!

APPENDICES

Appendix A:
Research Paper

Here is a research paper that I wrote during the summer after my junior year in high school. It was selected as one of the top five papers at the 2004 Research Science Institute in Caltech (RSI-Caltech) and won second place at the state Junior Science and Humanities Symposium.

Regulation of Late-Stage Flower Development by Downstream Genes of the Homeotic Protein AGAMOUS

Jerry Guo

under the direction of
Dr. Toshiro Ito and Professor Elliot Meyerowitz
Division of Biology
California Institute of Technology

Abstract

The genes and pathways AG regulates in late-stage flower development are largely unknown. Several putative downstream genes of AG involved in anther dehiscence were identified, including DAD1, MYB26, OPR3, COI1, and RBR1, through a bioinformatics approach. A 35S::AG-GR inducible line was constructed for timed-induction expression analysis of anther dehiscence versus indehiscence, which revealed the likely direct induction of DAD1 by AG. Mutated AG binding sites of DAD1 and MYB26 were linked to the β-glucuronidase reporter gene; the plasmid constructs were transformed into plants for GUS staining to test *in vivo* site activity. Results support the hypothesis that AG is continually functional and controls late-stage flower development by regulation of downstream genes.

1 Introduction

Floral organ development is a phenomenon that spatially and temporally involves the specific expression of a considerable number of genes in a variety of cascades and networks. Since the rise of the molecular age, much basic research has been devoted to elucidating the mechanisms and functions of and relationships between these homeotic genes [1]. Fortunately, because the evolutionary process provides relative physiological and biochemical similarity in plants, fundamental discoveries on the model organism *Arabidopsis thaliana* can be widely applied to all 25,000 flowering species. *Arabidopsis* not only produces a large number of seeds in a short generational period, but its entire genome has also been sequenced and mutant lines can be established [2].

1.1 Floral Organ Structure

Angiosperm eudicots develop flowers to produce gametophytes. The flower consists of four concentric whorls of organs: (1) sepals, (2) petals, (3) stamens, and (4) carpels, that sequentially form inward from the floral meristem. Stamens, the male reproductive organ, and carpels, the female counterpart that holds the ovules, produce sporogenous cells around floral stage 5. The stamen consists of an anther, the site of pollen development, and a stalk-like filament that aids in pollen dispersal. At floral stage 14, the flower opens and anther dehisces to release the mature pollen [3].

1.2 Developmental Model

The unifying principle in the flower-development field is the ABC model, which is applicable to a wide range of species. Three classes of homeotic selector genes that encode transcription factors (termed A, B, and C) determine floral organ identity combinatorially. Class-A genes alone specify sepals, A and B together specify petals, B and C together specify stamens, and C alone specifies carpels. In addition, classes A and C are mutually repressive. In general, gene products are expressed in floral regions that exhibit defects in mutants. The resulting transcription factors regulate floral development through a hierarchy of downstream targets [4].

Figure 1: *Arabidopsis* plants ready for tissue sampling or mutant selection [5]

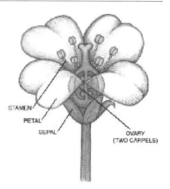

Figure 2: Four components of a flower [5]

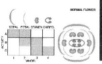 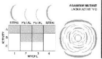

Figure 3: Flower structure of wild-type and AG mutant, as explained by the ABC model [5]

AGAMOUS, a class-C gene that encodes a transcription factor of the MADS-box family, plays a central role in flower development. The MADS-box family transcription factors bind to a target DNA sequence, the CArG box, as dimers. Since AG is responsible for reproductive organ development, mutants have a whorl pattern of sepal-petal-petal-sepal. The processes, mechanisms, and genes involved in differentiating whorl 3 and 4 primordia by AG into stamens and carpels are largely unknown [5].

1.3 Late-stage Regulatory Genes in Stamen Development

Like any other developmental process, a hierarchy of genes regulates anther dehiscence. During this late stage, programmed cell death ruptures the stomium; the tapetum and middle layer degenerates; the endothecial layer expands, and connective cells form fibrous bands. A lipid-derived signaling compound found in many plant species, jasmonic acid, was recently discovered to be actively involved in the control of anther dehiscence and male gametophyte development [3].

Three genes directly regulate this pathway and hence late-stage floral development. The *DEFECTIVE IN ANTHER DEHISCENCE1 (DAD1)* gene catalyzes the first step of JA biosynthesis by encoding a phospholipase A1 [6]. *OPR3* encodes an isozyme of 12-oxophytodienoate reductase that reduces OPDA for JA biosynthesis [7]. Mutants of both genes are sterile but can be rescued by exogenous JA. The JA signal transduction gene *COI1* encodes an F-box protein insensitive to JA treatment [8,9].

On the other hand, *MYB26* controls the mechanical rather than the biochemical aspect of anther dehiscence. Mutants produce fertile pollen when mechanically released from the anthers. Therefore, not only does the gene directly regulate late-stage development, it is also a valuable tool for manipulating male sterility. However, the endothecial layer lacks wall fortifications and does not shrink, which is necessary for retraction of the anther wall. The gene encodes a putative R2R3-type MYB transcription factor that activates the phenylpropanoid pathway to provide lignin residues for wall thickening [10].

1.4 Purpose and Significance

The genes and developmental processes that AG regulates throughout reproductive-organ development are in large part still left to be discovered. A key question to be answered is: does AG, which represents a typical plant homeotic protein, act as a switch that activates various developmental processes which then proceed without its expression, or does AG continually need to be expressed? In animals, the latter tends to be true, as illustrated by the *Drosophilia Ultrabithorax (UBX)* homeotic gene [11].

The question leads to two extreme hypotheses on how AG functions. One is that AG triggers a few genes at the top of a cascade during floral development, and in turn these AG targets regulate other genes. However, other than SHATTERPROOF2, no putative target genes of AG are known. The second possibility that is explored in this study is that AG directly and continually regulates the expression of many genes with different functions that act throughout reproductive-organ development.

Since AG has been recently implicated in microsporogenesis, an early-stage developmental process [12], it is essential to determine the expression and regulation of downstream AG genes in late-stage development in order to validate the second hypothesis. Therefore, this research will identify and explore the relationships of downstream genes of AG that regulate anther dehiscence, a late-stage developmental process. In particular, this study will determine whether the downstream genes are direct or indirect targets of AG.

AG has homologs in a variety of plant species, many of which are of great economic interest, and also in humans as oncogenes involved in the onset of cancer. Because 80% of plant food consists of flower components and only 50% of the genetic potential has been achieved, the research holds significant applications to improving food yield, genetically engineered crops, and breeding programs. At the basic-science level, the findings will also help elucidate the general behavior of plant homeotic proteins and further the floral developmental model [2].

2 Materials and Methods

2.1 AG-Inducible System

To reveal downstream processes of AG, a strain with AG-inducible activity was constructed. This strain was homozygous for the *ag-1*-null mutation and transgenic for 35S::AG-GR, a promoter-driven constitutive AG gene with a fusion at the carboxyterminal to the steroid-binding domain of the rat glucocorticoid receptor. This genotype of *ag-1* mutants results in flowers with an indefinite sepal-petal-petal whorl pattern [13].

However, continual treatment with dexamethasone (DEX), a steroid hormone, leads to a translocation from the cytoplasm to the nucleus of the fusion protein. The resulting flower has functional stamens and carpels and resembles the *35S::AG* plants, which implies that the AG-GR fusion protein can function as a normal AG protein. On the other hand, a single treatment with DEX only partially rescues the phenotype as flowers contain petals with stamenoid structures.

2.2 Plant Materials and Treatments

All plants were grown at 22°C under constant illumination in the Landsberg *erecta* background. Transgenic plants were generated by *Agrobacterium*-mediated infiltration. The 35S::AG-GR construct was transformed into wild-type plants and the primary T1 transformants were screened by basta selection. Phenotypic analyses in the *ag-1* were performed in the T1 generation, as well as in the T2 generation that was produced by selfing *ag-1/+* T1 plants.

2.3 AG Downstream Genes and Binding Site Identification

A review of previous research identified several genes directly implicated in anther dehiscence. To determine if these genes are downstream of AG requires the identification of putative AG binding sites to the gene

Regulation of Late-Stage Flower Development

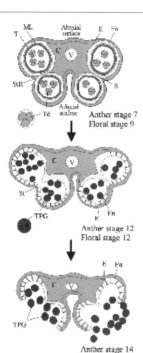

Figure 4: Cross-section of anthers at different stages.
[1]C, connective; E, epidermis; En, endothecium; ML, middle layer; S, septum; St, stomium; StR, stomium region; T, tapetum; Td, tetrads; TPG, tricellular pollen grains; V, vascular bundle [3]

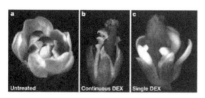

Figure 5: Phenotypic effects of *35S::AG-GR* induction

promoter. The genomic region of each identified gene was examined for the 16–base-pair perfect and weak consensus binding sequences of AG, which contains the 10-bp 'CArG-box core' (5'-CCNN(A/T)4GG-3') [14].

2.4 Timed-Induction Gene Expression Assay

Ag-1 35S::AG-GR plants were DEX treated (10 μM DEX, 0.015% Silwet L-77) either four times to induce AG and anther dehiscence or three times to observe indehiscence, in one-day intervals starting at stage 3. Inflorescence containing floral buds were collected from stage 8 to stage 13. RNA was isolated and purified from tissue samples of two independent sets by the RNeasy Mini Kit (Qiagen). Total RNA was reverse-transcribed to synthesize cDNA for RT-PCR by the ThermoScript RT-PCR system (Invitrogen).

The induction of the identified genes DAD1, MYB26, OPR3, COI1, RBR1, and a lipase control was tested through transcriptional expression levels in semiquantitative polymerase chain reaction with reverse transcription (RT-PCR) using primers DAD1-5', DAD1-3', MYB26-5', MYB26-3', OPR3-5', OPR3-3', COI1-5', COI1-3', RBR1-5', RBR-4', LIPASE-5', and LIPASE-3' after 42, 26, 28, 28, 28, and 24 cycles, respectively. Electrophoresis gel was run on the PCR products to measure the level of gene expression.

2.5 35S::AG-GR Construct

The coding region of AG was amplified from inflorescence cDNA and cloned into a blunt-ended EcoRI site of pBluescript SK (Stratagene) to produce pSK-AG. To produce pSK-AG-GR, pSK-AG was digested with EcoRI, filled in, and ligated with a DNA fragment containing a rat glucocorticoid hormone binding domain, which was excised with BamHI and XbaI from pRS020 (pDeltaGRBX) and filled in. The AG-Gr fragment was released from pSK-AG-GR by digestion with XbaI and ClaI and ligated into the corresponding sites of the binary vector pMAT137 that contains tandem cauliflower mosaic virus 35S enhancers and a terminator.

2.6 Plasmid Reporter-Gene Construct and Mutagenesis

The GUS-DAD1-5' construct was produced by first amplifying the coding region of the 3.5 kb genomic

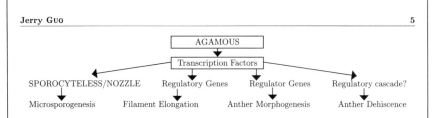

Figure 6: The "switch" hypothesis with late-stage functions unknown

sequence comprising DAD1 and the flanking intergenic sequences from inflorescence cDNA using primers DAD1-5'A20 and DAD1-5'B. UltraPfu High-Fidelity DNA polymerase (Stratagene) and wild-type Columbia genomic DNA were used through PCR at an extension time of 4 minutes and then cloned into the pENTR vector and subsequently into pBG-WFS7 for basta selection. An additional construct was further mutagenized by reversing the CArG-box core sequence CC...GG with the primers DAD1-5'MA and DAD1-5'MB and corrected to the perfect consensus with DAD1-5MCA and DAD1-5MCB using the QuikChange II XL Site-Directed Mutagenesis Kit (Stratagene).

The MYB26 promoter cloning was accomplished with amplification of the coding region by primers MYB26-5A2 and MYB26-5B at an extension time of 7 minutes. The fragment was cloned into pENTR, digested with Bst98I, blunt-ended with T4 DNA polymerase, and the GUS fragment was cut out with NarI, then blunt-ended with Klenow fragment, and finally ligated to produce the MYB26-GUS fusion. Further mutagenized and mutagenized to perfect AG-consensus sequence constructs were made by MYB26 mutagenesis primers. The MYB26-GUS fragment was then cloned into the pKGW gateway vector for plant transformation and selection. All plasmid constructs were sequenced using DAD1 primers 1–7 and MYB26 primers 1–19.

2.7   Western Blot

To check the timing of AG function, dynamic accumulation of AG-GR protein in the nuclei caused by repeated DEX treatments was examined. The ag-1 35S::AG-GR transgenic plants were treated once or 4 times with DEX, and the inflorescences were harvested at stage 1-10 after 3, 5, 7, 9, and 12 days. The crude nuclear extraction and purification were per-

formed according to previously published protocols (Ito, 1997). About 50 μg of crude nuclear extra was loaded onto the 7.5% Ready polyacrylamide gel (Biorad) and subsequently blotted onto the PVDF nylon membrane (Biograd). The AG-GR fusion protein was detected with AG-specific antibody using SuperSignal west dura extended duration substrate (Pierce). The band intensity was normalized with band intensities of small nuclear proteins by Memcode reversible protein stain kit for PVDF membranes (Pierce).

2.8   GUS Staining

Stage 8 to 13 inflorescences were rinsed and stained with x-gluc to determine β-glucuronidase activity for GUS expression analysis. Chlorophyll was removed by an ethanol series. Cleared whole-mount observation was performed according to published protocols.

3   Results

Figure 7 indicates that near-consensus AG binding sites were found on several putative downstream genes. In particular, the conserved core CArG-box sequence in the 5' promoter region of DAD1 is very close to the coding region, which makes the gene a likely candidate for AG binding. MYB26 also is a likely candidate since it has two near-consensus AG binding sites on each promoter region.

The idealized Graph 1 was based on the RT-PCR products shown in Figure 8, where a lipase derivative gene was the control. Four DEX treatments induced anther dehiscence and caused a peak in DAD1 expression around day 8, which thereafter gradually declined. Three DEX treatments resulted in a much lower expression level in DAD1, which quickly disappeared. MYB26 expression, independent of AG induction, reached a sharp peak around day 6 but also

6   Regulation of Late-Stage Flower Development

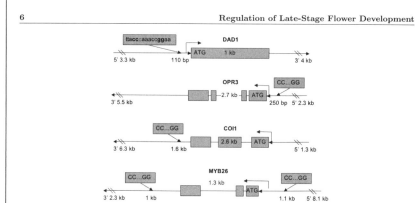

Figure 7: Sequence Schematics for Identified Putative AG Downstream Genes

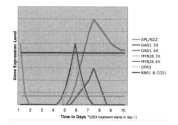

Graph 1. Timed-Induction Gene Expression

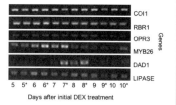

Days after initial DEX treatment

Figure 8: RT-PCR Expression Products. The asterisk denotes four DEX treatments, which ultimately cause anther dehiscence.

quickly disappeared. OPR3, RBR1, and COI showed no sign of change in expression level.

Figure 9 traces normal stamen development with prolonged AG induction. At the molecular level, four DEX treatments transferred enough AG-GR fusion protein into the nucleus where it stayed to cause anther dehiscence, as shown by Figure 10. Figure 11 focuses on the stage of anther dehiscence and reveals that the threshold for successful completion of development is four DEX treatments. Figure 12 illustrates the correct progression of flower development with AG induction.

4 Discussion

4.1 Timed-Induction Expression of Identified Regulatory Genes

The primary results, illustrated in Graph 1, of the AG timed-induction gene-expression assay reveals a substantial amount of interesting information about the relationship and functions of genes in the late-stage developmental pathway. This component of the study seeks to elucidate the effects of AG in late-stage development through an inducible system by examining the expression levels of various putative downstream genes when AG is turned on and off. First, when AG is induced, the SPOROCYTE-LESS/NOZZLE (SPL/NZZ) gene, which is responsible for microsporogenesis, is quickly expressed. The early, rapid induction and subsequent dramatic decline in SPL/NZZ expression implicates AG in early-stage development.

The remaining genes all regulate anther dehiscence, a late-stage developmental pathway. A pronounced difference in expression levels of DAD1 is evident between AG-induced anther dehiscence and indehiscence. The difference can be attributed to the three versus four DEX treatments. In other words, AG induction is responsible for the subsequent induction of DAD1, which supports the hypothesis of prolonged AG regulation in flower development. When AG induction is not strong enough to regulate anther dehiscence, downstream expression of DAD1 reaches a small peak shortly before the stage when anther dehiscence occurs and then quickly disappears. However, when AG does induce anther dehiscence through regulation of DAD1, DAD1 expression levels climb to a much higher peak and only drop slightly. The continued expression of DAD1 implies the necessary prolonged induction of AG for anther dehiscence to occur.

On the other hand, the MYB26 gene does not respond to a change in AG induction, as indicated by very similar expression levels between three and four DEX treatments. However, at this point, the results reveal earlier expression of MYB26 than DAD1, even though both regulate the anther-dehiscence pathway. The difference between the two genes is evidence that they are involved in separate regulatory cascades. Since the RNA expression assayed inflorescences were collected in bulk across various stages of development, differences in expression levels could be overshadowed. Thus, results from the GUS staining, which reveals gene activity spatially and temporally for individual inflorescences, must be analyzed before MYB26 can be classified as a direct, indirect, or non–AG-downstream target.

Additionally, OPR3, RBR1, and COI1 do not seem to be transcriptionally regulated at all due to the uniform levels in expression, which is in line with the negative lipase control, shown in Figure 8. Since the genes are involved in intermediate steps of various developmental pathways, it is logical that they would be continually expressed unless a homeotic regulator turns off the entire pathway. The lack of AG dependency in MYB26, OPR3, RBR1, and COI1 support the working hypothesis that AG specifically regulates certain genes in late-stage development. In this case, AG is on top of the anther dehiscence regulatory hierarchy and likely controls DAD1 as a direct target.

4.2 Phenotypic Duration Analysis

Phenotypes of AG-induced inflorescences were also examined in addition to exploring late-stage developmental relationships and functions at the molecular level. Figure 9 reveals that normal reproductive-organ development, especially in the late stages, requires continued AG induction. Prolonged AG activity throughout floral development indicates that AG actively functions in and even controls late-stage pathways. Prolonged AG activity can be seen in Figure 10, which shows the continued presence of the homeotic protein AG-GR fusion in the nucleus when induced. During anther indehiscence, there is no AG activity, as the fusion proteins quickly dissipated in the first few days, which means all downstream pathways are shut down, also illustrated by the expression assay. Therefore, the phenotypic results logically justify the molecular findings that AG controls anther dehiscence by direct regulation of downstream genes.

Furthermore, Figure 11 and 12 indicate that anther dehiscence occurs between the third and fourth DEX treatments. Obviously, no DEX treatment results in no AG induction and therefore no stamen development at all, reflective of the *ag-1* mutant. The fact that more than three DEX treatments are needed for anther dehiscence is evidence that AG is deeply involved in that developmental pathway. In addition, since just one treatment difference days after initial induction determines whether development completes successfully, AG is a critical regulator that controls a cascade of other regulatory genes in late-stage development, and the absence of AG has been seen to have far-reaching consequences during those stages.

5 Conclusions

5.1 Late-Stage Developmental Hierarchy

This study revealed that AGAMOUS is indeed functional in late-stage flower development. In particular, AGAMOUS was shown to directly control anther dehiscence through regulation of the downstream gene

8   Regulation of Late-Stage Flower Development

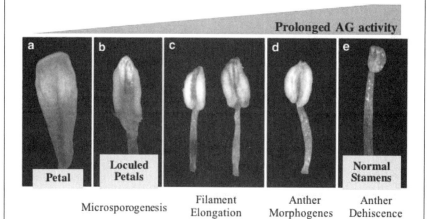

Figure 9: Continued AG Function Throughout Development

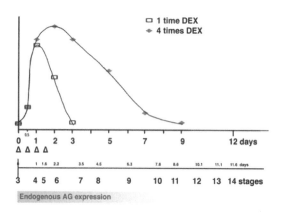

Figure 10: Extended Localization of AG-GR Fusion Protein in Nucleus

DAD1. AG putatively binds to the near-consensus site on the 5' promoter region of DAD1, identified by genomic analysis, resulting in elevated levels of DAD1 expression that ultimately causes anther dehiscence.

On the other hand, MYB26 has two near-consensus AG binding sites, but the timed-induction expression assay gave no proof that the regulatory gene is a direct downstream target of AG. However, MYB26 was shown to be expressed earlier than DAD1 even though it also directly controls anther dehiscence. Therefore, it is probable that MYB26 is involved in an AG-dependent late-stage developmental pathway. Results also provided the evidence that OPR3, COI1, and RBR1 are not transcriptionally regulated due to uniform levels of expression.

5.2 Necessity of Prolonged AG Induction for Flower Development

On a more general level, prolonged AG activity was found to be necessary for late-stage development of normal stamens, although endogenous expression levels did decrease over time, which implies dependence on more complex hierarchies involving indirect targets in late-stage development. AG was also phenotypically observed through the inducible system to be required for anther dehiscence. Therefore, the molecular and phenotypic evidence illustrated the direct control of late-stage development by AG through a regulatory hierarchy. In turn, the results also support the second hypothesis that AG directly and continually regulates the expression of many genes with different functions that act throughout reproductive-organ development.

5.3 Future Work

Although the research expanded on the developmental model, much more work needs to be devoted to revealing the relationship and functions of these regulatory genes. Results from the GUS staining of the plasmid constructs, which should come in within a couple months, will more clearly indicate whether these downstream genes are direct or indirect targets of AG *in vivo*, in addition to determining their spatial expression. The downstream genes that were classified as AG-dependent by current results could still turn out to be direct targets since samples will be analyzed individually. Chromatin immunoprecipitation will also be conducted to observe the physical binding of AG to the identified binding sites. Finally, genome-wide microarray analysis can be conducted to identify more downstream genes of AG that regulate late-stage development since the current research has illustrated how a plant homeotic protein functions throughout development.

5.4 Acknowledgments

I would like to thank my mentors, Dr. Toshiro Ito, Senior Research Scientist, and Professor Meyerowitz, Division of Biology Chair, for their continued support, guidance, and inspiration. I would also like to thank my tutor, Jacqueline Choi, and fellow students, staff, and lab members for their invaluable help with the research paper and presentation. I greatly appreciate the opportunity provided by the Center for Excellence in Education to conduct research through the 2004 Research Science Institute.

References

[1] H. Yu, T. Ito, Y. Zhao, J. Peng, P. Kumar, and E.M. Meyerowitz. Floral homeotic genes are targets of gibberellin signaling in flower development. Proceedings of the National Academy of Science 101 (2004), no. 20, 7827–7832.

[2] S. Harris. *Arabidopsis*—map makers of the plant kingdom. Available at http://www.nsf.gov/od/lpa/news/publicat/nsf0050/arabidopsis/arabidopsis.htm (2004/07/30).

[3] R.J. Scott, M. Spielman, and H.G. Dickinson. Stamen structure and function. The Plant Cell 16 (2004), S46–S60.

[4] E. Meyerowitz. The genetics of flower development. Scientific American (November 1994), 56–65.

[5] T. Jack. Molecular and genetic mechanisms of floral control. The Plant Cell 16 (2004), S1–S17.

[6] S. Ishiguro, A. Kawai-Oda, J. Ueda, I. Nishida, and K. Okada. The *DEFECTIVE IN ANTHER DEHISCENCE1* gene encodes a novel phospholipase A1 catalyzing the initial step of jasmonic acid biosynthesis, which synchronizes pollen maturation, anther dehiscence, and flower opening in *Arabidopsis*. The Plant Cell 13 (2001), 2191–2209.

[7] A. Stintzi and J. Browse. The *Arabidopsis* male-sterile mutant, opr3, lacks the 12-oxophytodienoic acid reductase required for jasmonate synthesis. Proceedings of the National Academy of Science 97 (2000), no. 19, 10625–10630.

10   Regulation of Late-Stage Flower Development

Figure 11: Timed-Induction Floral Phenotypes

Figure 12: AG-Induced (4× DEX) Inflorescences in Different Stages

AGAMOUS

SPOROCYTELESS/NOZZLE	Regulatory Genes	Regulatory Genes	DAD1	MYB26
Microsporogenesis	Filament Elongation	Anther Morphogenesis	COI1, OPR3	
			Anther Dehiscence	

Figure 13: The "continued" hypothesis of AG function in late-stage development

[8] B.J.F. Feys, C.E. Benedetti, C.N. Penfold, and J.G. Turner. *Arabidopsis* mutants selected for resistance to the phytotoxin coronatine are male sterile, insensitive to methyl jasmonate, and resistant to a bacterial pathogen. The Plant Cell 6 (1994), 751–759.

[9] D. Xie, B.F. Feys, S. James, M. Nieto-Rostro, and J.G. Turner. *COI1*: An *Arabidopsis* gene required for jasmonate-regulated defense and fertility. Science 280 (1998), 1091-1094

[10] S. Steiner-Lange, U.S. Unte, L. Eckstein, C. Yang, Z.A. Wilson, E. Schmelzer, K. Dekker, and H. Saedler. Disruption of *Arabidopsis thaliana MYB26* results in male sterility due to non-dehiscent anthers. The Plant Journal 34 (2003), 519–528.

[11] J. Riechmann. *The* Arabidopsis *book*. The American Society of Plant Biologists, Rockville, MD (2002).

[12] T. Ito, F. Wellmer, H. Yu, P. Das, N. Ito, M. Alves-Ferreira, J.L. Riechmann, and E.M. Meyerowitz. The homeotic protein AGAMOUS controls microsporogenesis by regulation

of SPOROCYTELESS. Nature 430 (2004), 356–360.

[13] T. Ito, H. Sakai, and E.M. Meyerowitz. Whorl-specific expression of the SUPERMAN gene of *Arabidopsis* is mediated by *cis* elements in the transcribed region. Current Biology 13 (2003), no. 17, 1524–1530.

[14] H. Yu, T. Ito, F. Wellmer, and E.M. Meyerowitz. Repression of AGAMOUS-LIKE 24 is a crucial step in promoting flower development. Nature Genetics 36 (2004), no. 2, 157–161.

Appendix B:
Articles

Targeted therapy to aid cancer patients
New radiation therapy is less dangerous

By Jerry Guo
Contributing Reporter
Yale Daily News, **September 7, 2005**

Siri Lynn, a marketing consultant from Fairfield, Conn., had a friend diagnosed with breast cancer two years ago. Recently, Lynn said, she developed breast cancer herself and was referred to Yale-New Haven Hospital by her friend. Now, she is the first Connecticut patient enrolled in a clinical trial for a novel breast cancer treatment at the hospital.

Dr. Joanne Weidhaas is co-coordinating the Yale effort as part of an international study on an emerging treatment called accelerated partial breast irradiation. The little-known procedure, which has been around for more than 10 years, will be compared in effectiveness to traditional whole breast irradiation by the ongoing study.

"[The research is] a change in paradigm. The question is, do we need to treat the entire breast?" Weidhaas said.

Whether this alternative treatment will work as well as traditional methods is an area of controversy, she said.

Although both methods are relatively safe, PBI treatment lasts only five days, while whole breast irradiation takes as long as six weeks. The twice daily PBI sessions take just minutes and minimize radiation exposures to healthy tissue. The study, funded by the National Cancer Institute, is being conducted at 150 sites and involves 3,000 women.

Weidhaas, a professor of therapeutic radiology at the Yale School of Medicine, is responsible for reviewing the protocol, selecting patients and collecting data.

Now in phase-three clinical trials, one step away from FDA approval, Weidhaas said the treatment seeks to strike a balance between killing a tumor and hurting the surrounding tissue.

She said 40 percent of women with breast cancer choose to have radical mastectomies rather than take time off for the lengthy standard radiation treatment. Additionally, 25 percent of women who had a lumpectomy skip the subsequent radiation, Weidhaas said, which is critical to eradicating any cancerous traces.

By cutting treatment time down to one week, PBI gives women more options, she said; however, the treatment is not for everybody.

"There's still a place for whole breast irradiation," said Dr. Bruce Haffty, professor of radiology at the Medical School and breast cancer program director. "But now is the time to put it to the final test."

Haffty said the Medical School has several other breast cancer clinical trials on the table and is continually finding ways to improve radiation and examine cancer dynamics at the molecular level.

"As long as you have a general idea, then there are opportunities for advancement," said Renard Walker, a breast cancer researcher at the National Cancer Institute.

Walker said the Yale team has had much success but much more needs to be done.

Patricia Spicer, breast cancer program coordinator at the nonprofit support organization Cancer Care, said that even with initial success, it will take a while for the general public to accept PBI. Currently only a few patients even know about this alternative treatment, so the underlying demand is not great, she said.

Yet for those who do have access to such clinical studies, the rewards can be great. Lynn said she was very lucky to hear about the study and has complete faith in the Yale investigators.

"From the parking attendant to doctors, it has been an awesome experience," she said.

A Strategy That Works: Hook 'Em While They're Young

By Jerry Guo
Science, **July 14, 2006**

A groundbreaking program is giving Chinese high schoolers a chance to try their hand in a university lab—and audition for roles in China's innovation drive

SHANGHAI—While his friends were babysitting or waiting tables, 18-year-old Jim Liu spent his summer vacation last year in Boston, developing software that allows children to construct LEGO Mindstorms robots able to do everything from play soccer to dispense candy. Liu, a native of Shanghai, was one of 88 teenagers from across the world selected for the Research Science Institute (RSI), an all-expenses-paid summer program at the Massachusetts Institute of Technology (MIT). Now back home, Liu is hoping some of the excitement he felt will rub off on fellow teens in China. He's a counselor with the inaugural RSI-China, which began last week here at Fudan University and will run through 15 August.

The program is trailblazing in other ways: It's the first time a Chinese university has partnered with a U.S. organization to sponsor a high-school program. Run by the Center for Excellence in Education (CEE), a nonprofit organization based in McLean, Virginia, and Fudan University, RSI-China aims to build on the success of its flagship MIT program to train innovative young Chinese minds. "High-school students bring a new perspective [to the lab] and a new discovery is even possible," says Lu Fang, physics dean at Fudan and co-director of RSI-China.

For 6 weeks, 35 of the brightest high-school juniors in Shanghai will experience a reprieve from cramming for university entrance exams to work in Fudan labs. They will also attend classes and lectures on hot research areas. Half the Shanghai staff are graduates of the MIT program. RSI-China culminates with students presenting findings in talks and undergraduate-level term papers. This format has worked well for RSI-MIT, which has had an impressive track record over its 23-year lifetime for hooking students on science: Some 80 percent of alumni have gone on to graduate school in the sciences.

Following the success of similar programs in Boston, Bulgaria, Israel and Singapore, CEE sought a foothold in China and got a warm welcome from the government. A philanthropist steered CEE to Fudan, where university administrators were eager to host RSI-China. They see it as a way to hold on to some of Shanghai's top students, many of whom end up in Beijing at Qinghua University or Beijing University. To bankroll the program's first year, organizers signed up local backers: Shanghai Educational Press Group and Shanghai Wall Street Advisors.

RSI-China applicants faced stiff competition. More than 30 schools across Shanghai nominated their top 10 students, although the program could accommodate only 10 percent of this elite pool. CEE staff interviewed each student to find those with a passion for science outside the classroom, Lu says.

Fudan professors say they welcome the opportunity to work with talented high schoolers. "It's a very good idea. They can already start doing interesting stuff," says Rudolf Fleischer, a computer scientist at Fudan who has volunteered to mentor one student on a project employing computational geometry to improve optical character recognition. "My goal is to show them what happens at university, because if you start early, you get better students," Fleischer says. For many Chinese professors, he adds, mentoring is a new skill: "Traditional Chinese education is based on memorizing. Mentoring is not a concept that many Chinese professors understand well."

RSI-China is a small step toward addressing a widespread shortcoming of Chinese schools: Few offer hands-on science instruction, let alone lab facilities. "This is a very different concept for educating students in China," says CEE President Joann DiGennaro. The main aim in Chinese schools is to hone test-taking skills, says Liu. After RSI, he says, "creativity will be activated. Now, all that high-school students seem to think about is the entrance exam, and that's not good." After spending the 2004-05 academic year as an exchange student at T. C. Williams High School in Alexandria, Virginia, Qian Yingzhi, a member of RSI-China's inaugural class, says she appreciates the rare invitation to work in a Chinese lab. "I want to expand my horizons," she says.

The projects are "real research that we undertake every day," says Yang Zhong, executive dean of life sciences at Fudan. He is hosting a student who will fish flavonoid genes out of Tibetan plants as part of a project to detect adaptation through molecular evolution. Other projects include working on solar energy cells, examining the nonlinear behavior of yeast cells zapped with electrical currents and screening for microbes that break down pollutants.

The grand challenge of RSI-China is to facilitate the exchange of ideas with the international community, says Lu. "China is an emerging world power in academics," adds DiGennaro. She hopes the program will be able to improve international relations between China and the United States while teaching students to think on their own. Lu agrees that this is a worthwhile aim. "We don't want the professor to teach the student but rather the student to teach himself," he says.

Lu has lofty aspirations for RSI-China. If all goes well this summer, he hopes that next year the program can recruit students from across the country. For Liu, the taste of real research last summer impelled him to pursue a science career in the United States; as a first step on that journey, he is enrolling at MIT this fall. He hopes the experience will be equally motivating for RSI-China's freshman class. At least it will be a refreshing break from having to memorize their science textbooks.

The Galápagos Islands Kiss Their Goat Problem Goodbye

Jerry Guo
Science, September 15, 2006

The world's largest eradication campaign has virtually rid an ecological wonderland of feral goats, a devastating invader. Next in the crosshairs: cats and rats

SANTA CRUZ, GALÁPAGOS ISLANDS—Rachel Atkinson hops like a Darwin finch from one volcanic outcropping to the next, then plunges into ankle-deep mud. Squishing as she walks, the botanist with the Charles Darwin Research Station homes in on the ailing invaders: blackberry, passion fruit and quinine bushes clustered near Santa Cruz Island's last shrubby stands of Scalesia trees. Atkinson smiles in approval. One more blast of herbicide ought to prevent the aliens from regrowing and give the Scalesia a shot at survival after all.

Atkinson's search-and-destroy mission is part of an ambitious 6-year, $18 million Global Environment Facility (GEF) effort by the station and Galápagos National Park to turn the tide against invasive species in the Galápagos Islands, the fragile crucible of life that inspired Charles Darwin to formulate his theory of evolution 150 years ago. The GEF grant runs until next year, but the results so far are stunning. A survey here last month has confirmed that enemy number one—the feral goat—has been virtually wiped off Isabela, Santiago and Pinta islands. All told, some 140,000 feral goats were slain in 5 years of the GEF-funded Project Isabela, the largest eradication project ever undertaken. "A great battle has been won here," says Victor Carrion, subdirector of the park.

Although one bane has been eliminated, others are at large. In northern Isabela, rats have ravaged the last two nesting sites of mangrove finches, estimated at fewer than 100. And both rats and feral cats have decimated a subspecies of marine iguana (Amblyrhynchus cristatus albemarlensis) endemic to Isabela, prompting the World Conservation Union to add it to its vulnerable list in 2004. Rangers have set out traps and poison for Isabela's rats and are plotting eradication campaigns on Floreana and Santiago islands. An effort to poison feral cats will commence next year.

The Galápagos have been under siege ever since pirates and whalers began visiting the archipelago in the 1700s and leaving behind goats, pigs and other animals as a living larder for future visits. But it wasn't until the late 1980s that the goat population suddenly started booming, possibly due to El Niño-driven changes in vegetation patterns. Godfrey Merlen, a Galápagos native and director of WildAid, says he saw "two or three" goats on the upper flanks of Isabela's Alcedo volcano in 1992. When he returned 3 years later, he saw hundreds. "It was total chaos," Merlen says. The goats had denuded the once-lush terrain, transforming brush and cloud forests into patchy grassland.

Ecological shock waves rippled across Isabela. The highlands had served as a safe haven for species such as the giant tortoise. "We saw many more tortoises falling into the volcanic craters," trying to reach feeding grounds or because of erosion, says Carrion. "Being a baby tortoise is hard enough," adds Thomas Fritts, past president of the Charles Darwin Foundation. "Competing with voracious herbivores is an extra challenge."

Park rangers quickly caught on and started slaying the goats in 1995. They had eradicated a much smaller population from Española Island in the 1970s. But with tens of thousands of goats on northern Isabela alone, officials knew they needed a novel approach. In 2000, GEF agreed to bankroll an antigoat operation as long as it was part of an effort to tackle invasive species across the board (*Science*, 27 July 2001, p. 590).

Goats were still top priority. The park imported hunting dogs from New Zealand and trained them to track and kill goats. Helicopters were pressed into service for sharpshooters to reach rugged highlands. To flush out the last feral holdouts, the park released "Judas" goats, including sterilized females plied with hormones to keep them in heat and attract males. The last feral goat in northern Isabela was shot in March. Hunters have also purged pigs from Santiago and donkeys from both islands.

Local scientists say native plants are already bouncing back. Seedlings of Scalesia and soldierbush are sprouting on Alcedo. And on Santiago, cat's claw and Galápagos guava are thriving, providing nesting grounds for the secretive Galápagos rail.

One looming threat is microbial invaders. "What can cause far greater and permanent damage are the small introduced species [such as] West Nile virus, now in Colombia, a stone's throw away from Galápagos," says Merlen. In a paper in the August issue of *Conservation Biology*, Marm Kilpatrick of the Consortium for Conservation Medicine in New York City and colleagues concluded that West Nile virus-ridden mosquitoes could easily hitch a ride on a commercial jet from mainland Ecuador. "The Galápagos has been very lucky so far, but it's just a matter of time," says Simon Goodman of the University of Leeds in the U.K., an author of the paper. He says that West Nile virus could inflict the sort of damage in the Galápagos that avian malaria did in Hawaii in 2004, when it drove a honeycreeper (Melamprosops phaeosoma) to extinction. Galápagos officials pledge to remain vigilant and point to the establishment in 2003 of a molecular pathology lab on Santa Cruz funded by the U.K.'s Darwin Initiative.

To avoid ceding hard-won breathing room for native species, the park and research station plan to set up a $15 million fund for ongoing eradication efforts. In the meantime, they are stepping up efforts against invasive plants and gearing up for the cat-and-rat blitzkrieg. Unless these and other unwelcome visitors go the way of the goats, warns Carrion, "the worst may be yet to come."

Chinese Gene Therapy: Splicing Out the West?

Jerry Guo and Hao Xin
Science, **November 24, 2006**

Chinese researchers have been the first to put cancer gene-therapy products on the market, but critics question the data behind the success stories

BEIJING—Maria Corina Roman, a Danish surgeon, made international news when she decided to seek treatment for her breast cancer using the world's first commercial gene therapy. Disappointed with standard cancer treatment, Roman flew to China in 2004 to try Gendicine, a Chinese product that contains a virus with a human tumor suppressor gene (p53) spliced into its DNA. Just days after the first injection, Roman reported that she had regained energy and appetite. Gendicine's maker, SiBiono GeneTech Co. in Shenzhen, spread the word. Encouraging reports about this gene therapy appeared in the *Financial Times, Business Week* and *China Daily*.

This fall, however, Roman's tumor has returned, SiBiono acknowledges. The company's chief executive, Peng Zhaohui, says nevertheless that the drug has proved to have "good efficacy," adding that Roman, SiBiono's most famous client, "should continue to treat with Gendicine."

Peng's advice is based on more than optimism; it reflects national policy. China's State Food and Drug Administration (SFDA) approved Gendicine for clinical use in October 2003 and licensed its commercial production in spring of 2004. Last year, SFDA approved a second genetically engineered anticancer product: a modified virus, dubbed H101, designed to infect and kill cells containing mutated versions of the p53 gene. The maker, Sunway Biotech Co. in Shanghai, says it expects to strike a licensing deal by the end of this year with Genzyme Corp. in Cambridge, Massachusetts, to run clinical trials of a Genzyme gene-therapy product in China and possibly test H101 in the United States.

As these projects advance in China, gene therapies in North America and Europe are struggling to complete premarket clinical tests. After a U.S. patient died in a 1999 gene therapy trial and two children in French trials developed leukemia in 2002, the U.S. Food and Drug Administration (FDA) tightened controls on experiments, says James Norris, head of the U.K.-based International Society for Cell & Gene Therapy of Cancer. Western companies say they are making progress but have not yet brought a single gene therapy to market.

Some see this as a sign that China is catching up with, or even surpassing, the West. "I think the future of gene therapy will be in China," says Andre Lieber, a gene therapy researcher at the University of Washington (UW), Seattle. But he warns that recent claims of success should be read with caution. There is a "problem" with interpreting clinical studies done in China, Lieber says. Often the primary data are published only in Chinese—raising a barrier to nonspeakers—and even when they appear in English, critical information may be missing.

Intellectual-property rights may be problematic, too. Some researchers in the West have questioned claims of independent innovations made by Chinese drug companies; this could limit sales outside China. Finally, critics argue that the Chinese regulatory system is not rigorous and that Gendicine, for one, was approved with scant evidence of efficacy. With drugs to treat cancer, "the bar is a lot lower than in the United States to get approval," says Frank McCormick, director of the University of California, San Francisco, Comprehensive Cancer Center.

High hopes

On a plot of land in the outskirts of Shenzhen stands an empty building with opaque windows, a site where owners hope a biotech bonanza will blossom. Starting next year, this newly constructed plant will begin producing 1.5 million vials of

Gendicine per year, seven times the capacity of SiBiono's current facility, according to SiBiono's Peng. *Science* visited Peng in his office in May and spoke with him last month by phone.

A hallway at the company's headquarters is plastered with clippings from Chinese and international media describing how Gendicine has helped cancer patients. Peng said SiBiono aims to spearhead the sale of gene-therapy products in China with Gendicine. It was given its Chinese name—jin you sheng, "born again today"— by China's Vice President Zeng Qinghong when he made a ceremonial visit to the company a month before SFDA cleared the drug for market.

SFDA approved Gendicine as a treatment for head and neck cancer based on small clinical trials showing that more patients had tumors disappear with Gendicine plus radiotherapy (64 percent) than with radiotherapy alone (19 percent). Peng has called these "phase II/III" trials, an unusual term that combines safety (phases I and II) with proof of efficacy (phase III).

In 2005, SFDA approved Sunway's H101, also designed for treatment of head and neck cancer, after a 160-patient phase III clinical trial showed that 74 percent of patients receiving H101 plus chemotherapy experienced a reduction in the size of tumors compared to 40 percent of patients receiving chemotherapy alone.

Gendicine has now been given to more than 4,000 patients to treat not just head and neck tumors but also 50 different cancers, Peng claims. The venture thus far has received about $6 million in grants and government start-up funds as well as $6 million from private investors.

Peng projected in 2004 that 50,000 patients would have received Gendicine treatment by the end of 2006. Demand is far short of that target, but if the drug works—and if patients can afford the high price of treatment, costing $1,680 to $3,360 per cycle—the market could eventually be huge. "Having 1.3 billion potential patients compared to 300 million in the United States makes a successful drug very lucrative in China," says Norris.

Imitation or innovation?

Doubts persist, however, about China's future as a gene-therapy powerhouse. Some U.S. companies allege that China's commercial products are spinoffs of Western inventions with relatively minor modifications. Introgen Therapeutics in Austin, Texas, for example, claims that SiBiono's Gendicine is similar to its own experimental product, a recombinant adenovirus containing the human p53 gene (rAd-p53).

Wei-Wei Zhang, president and CEO of San Diego-based GenWay Biotech, published the first paper on rAd-p53 while working at the University of Texas M. D. Anderson Cancer Center in Houston in 1994. He holds U.S. patents on the viral construct and related processes. M. D. Anderson negotiated a license with Introgen, which has spent more than $70 million to develop a product based on Zhang's rAd-p53, trademarked Advexin. It has been in clinical trials since 1994. The company's ongoing phase III trial using Advexin to treat head and neck cancer is under review for "accelerated approval" by FDA.

Introgen's 106-patient phase II trial in 2005 showed a 10 percent "tumor response rate," defined by at least 30 percent reduction in tumor size, in patients who received Advexin alone. Introgen Vice President Robert Sobol says phase III trials are going well.

Meanwhile, Introgen CEO David Nance claims that Gendicine is a "derivative" of his company's product. In an August 2006 filing with the U.S. Securities and Exchange Commission, Introgen claims that Gendicine infringes on a 1994 patent filed in China but concedes that "enforcement of patents in China is unpredictable, and we do not know if monetary damages could be recovered from SiBiono."

Peng disputes these statements. In a phone interview, he said that Gendicine is "very different" from Introgen's product and that the only similarity is the use of p53.

Sunway acknowledges that its product, H101, was inspired by U.S. research but says it developed H101 independently—a claim that is not disputed. According to Sunway officials and other observers, H101 is similar to a product called Onyx-015, made by Onyx Pharmaceuticals Inc. in San Francisco. Onyx-015 and H101 both use a modified adenovirus to target probable cancer cells that have a deficient or mutated p53 gene. This so-called oncolytic virus, which has been tested in U.S. phase I and II clinical trials, is designed to replicate in target cells and kill them.

Onyx never filed for a patent on Onyx-015 in China. Nevertheless, Sunway CEO Hu Fang says that in developing H101, "we followed almost everything Onyx did in clinical trials. ... We modified the virus, very little, for patent purposes."

Although Onyx-015 has shown in phase II trials that it also can achieve local shrinkage of head and neck tumors of about 60 percent to 70 percent, McCormick, a co-founder of Onyx, says this was not enough to win FDA approval. Regulators wanted more evidence, specifically data showing that Onyx-015 prolonged survival. Onyx ended a phase III trial when the main backer pulled out in 2005.

At this point, Sunway obtained exclusive worldwide rights from Onyx to use the 015 modified virus in H101. "We bought the patent from Onyx because now we want to put our drug in Europe, the United States and Japan," says Hu. The distribution network will be ready soon, and Hu expects 2,000 patients to sign up in the first year. The company is working on an improved version, H103, that includes a heat shock protein designed to attack metastatic tumors by inducing an immune response.

Different standards

The Chinese government is both an investor in and a regulator of biotech projects such as the ventures that produced Gendicine and H101. Some observers, including Norris, are concerned that the government's dual role could weaken its vigor as an enforcer of standards. He notes that "backers of these companies are high-level government officials." From 2001 to 2005, the Ministry of Science and Technology (MOST) provided $106 million to innovative drug development, some of which went to SiBiono.

SiBiono's Peng also helped write a regulatory guidebook for SFDA on evaluating cancer gene-therapy products. Leaning forward in his executive chair, Peng proudly shows off a thin pamphlet. "It's the most systematic guidelines in the world, and I was the main framer," Peng exclaims. There's an appearance of a conflict of interest in this, Norris says, although the government's acceptance of help with regulatory guidelines may reflect a wish to catch up quickly with standards in developed countries.

Peng acknowledges that SiBiono has government support and confirms that the application for Gendicine was sped "through a special channel." The data from the Gendicine trials were submitted to SFDA in March 2003; the drug was approved 7 months later. Sunway also "pushed" to get its H101 application through in 10 months, Hu confirms. But companies can also apply for accelerated review at the U.S. FDA, and Peng argues that Chinese companies must comply with strict regulations, just like their counterparts in the West.

Yin Hongzhang, SFDA's chief of biological products, says the agency has "special policies" to approve a drug on the fast track if an initial technical review looks fine. "But we would require the manufacturer to do further research and collect more data on efficacy to submit" after approval, he says. Earlier this year, he asked SiBiono to send the required follow-up data; when he spoke with *Science* he was still waiting for the data.

China's regulatory framework differs in another way. Whereas the U.S. FDA often requires that novel cancer drugs extend the life of the patient to be judged a success, SFDA approved both Gendicine and H101 on the basis of tumor shrinkage.

Sunway's Hu says his company intends to show that H101 increases survival as well as shrinks tumors. "Survival time for patients is very important," says Hu. In a retrospective study, he says the company has found that H101 can provide a 7-month survival benefit, but the results were not significant. They are now repeating phase III trials with a bigger sample size and more treatment cycles designed to maximize survival benefit.

There is good reason to expect that Chinese biotechnology will have a bright future. Companies in China "have excellent production facilities, a lot of money and a lot of good people," says UW's Lieber. Zhang adds that Chinese bioscientists deserve credit for picking up U.S. pioneers' work in cancer gene therapy.

At least a half-dozen Chinese gene-therapy drugs are in clinical trials at the moment, says Savio Woo, past president of the American Society of Gene Therapy. "Before the end of this decade, they should have more drugs. I will be surprised if they didn't," he says. China also may draw significant outside investment to the field.

Genzyme, for example, is negotiating to have Sunway run a phase II gene therapy clinical trial in China. The U.S. company is testing a modified adenovirus construct (Ad2/HIF-1) to promote angiogenesis in patients with peripheral arterial disease, an immobilizing condition that decreases blood flow to the muscles. Already, Genyzme has enrolled 300 patients in Europe and the United States. "The climate in China is changing, with more innovative companies not just focused on manufacturing," says Genzyme Vice President Earl Collier Jr. "We want to participate."

Zhang nevertheless worries about "media hype" that could "mislead patients, officials and investors and cause significant damage to the further development of China's biotech industry." He hopes China can avoid repeating the mistakes that set back gene therapy in the West.

River Dolphins Down for the Count, and Perhaps Out
Jerry Guo
Science, **December 22, 2006**

The world's rarest cetacean is nowhere to be found. Last week, a 3,500-kilometer survey along China's Yangtze River failed to turn up a single river dolphin, or baiji (Lipotes vexillifer). "It's going to take a rescue effort of epic proportions to save this species," says Karen Baragona, director of the World Wildlife Fund's China programs. But it may already be too late for the nearly blind, pale creature. Expedition organizer August Pfluger, head of the Swiss-based baiji.org Foundation, says bluntly: "The baiji is functionally extinct."

The gloomy appraisal has prompted researchers to redouble efforts to save another endangered Yangtze cetacean, the finless porpoise, known in China as the jiangzhu, or river pig. (Cetaceans include whales, dolphins and porpoises.) The survey recorded fewer than 300 of the world's only freshwater porpoise (Neophocaena phocaenoides asiaorientalis). Experts now estimate a total population of at most 1,400, a 50 percent decline from the last major survey in 1991. "Without further intervention, the finless porpoise will be the next baiji," says survey member Zhang Xianfeng of the Wuhan Institute of Hydrobiology.

Although biologists knew the baiji was scarce, coming home empty-handed after a 6-week survey up and down the Yangtze was unexpected. A team from China, the United Kingdom and the United States had planned to follow the survey with a $400,000 "rescue mission" to transfer any captured baiji to Tian-e-Zhou Lake in Hubei Province, a sanctuary holding 30 finless porpoises. That plan has been shelved, says Pfluger.

The baiji split from other dolphins 20 million years ago. Since then, the baiji's eyes have shrunk to pea size. It can discern only light and dark, so it relies on a finely tuned sonar to hunt prey in the silty Yangtze. The last comprehensive survey in 1997 found 13 baiji; from this figure, experts pegged the population at fewer than 100.

"For us to see zero means there might be 10" left in the wild, says survey member Barbara Taylor, a marine biologist with the U.S. National Oceanic and Atmospheric Administration (NOAA). Or, as Pfluger notes, zero may mean zero. If so, the baiji would follow the Stellar's sea cow, Caribbean monk seal and Japanese sea lion into oblivion as the fourth large marine mammal to go extinct in the last 3 centuries. It would be the first cetacean lost in modern times.

Although the baiji's fate is uncertain, the dangers it faces are all too apparent. The most immediate threat is the use of rolling hooks, says expedition co-director Robert Pitman, a NOAA marine biologist. These illegal fishing lines are stretched across a river and are known to snag and drown baiji. During the survey, says Pitman, "we saw hundreds of fishermen using rolling hooks."

Long-term hazards are pollution and choking boat traffic. Near Poyang Lake in Jiangxi Province, connected to the Yangtze by a narrow channel, Taylor counted some 1,200 boats in a span of 2 hours. Between the heavy traffic and numerous factories hard up against the lakeshore, Taylor declares Poyang the "biggest environmental disaster" she's ever seen. That's bad news, as Poyang, China's largest lake, is one of the last redoubts of the finless porpoise: It has the biggest intact population, estimated at 400, with 80 spotted during the survey. Plucking the porpoise from peril won't be simple. Proposed megadams may fragment remaining populations, says Zhang. "There's no hope to change the environmental conditions on the Yangtze," he says. Pfluger says his organization will educate fishers about the impact of illegal fishing and finance a sustainable-fishing initiative at Tian-e-Zhou Lake. There, two or three porpoises are born each year, and captive breeding has resulted in a pregnancy last year, says expedition co-director Wang Ding of the Institute of Hydrobiology. "We have to set up more seminatural reserves like Tian-e-Zhou," Wang says.

Sadly, that approach may no longer be applicable to the baiji, an apparent victim of China's booming economy and the attendant environmental degradation of a mighty river. "It seems the baiji is the only thing that is not made in China anymore," says Pitman.

Random Samples

By Jerry Guo
Science, May 4, 2007

Lonesome George, a Galápagos giant tortoise locally known as Solitario Jorge, is called the "rarest living creature" by Guinness World Records. After a futile worldwide search in zoos to find others from his home island of Pinta and failed efforts to get him to mate—including flying in a Swiss zoologist to extract some sperm—70-year-old George seemed destined to stay the last of his species.

Until now. A team of geneticists led by Adalgisa Caccone and Jeffrey Powell at Yale University report this week in *Current Biology* that, after analyzing DNA from

27 tortoises on neighboring Isabela Island, they've found a relative. One male turned out to be a cross between the native species (Geochelone becki) and George's (G. abingdoni). Caccone says she plans to lead a bigger expedition back to the Isabela Island turtle population—which may number up to 8,000—to sample 1,000 more. "Chances are quite high that there's a pure Pinta individual out there," says Caccone, which means hope yet for finding George a mate or even an extended family.

"It's good to have a positive story in our world of diminishing biodiversity," says Oliver Ryder, a geneticist at the San Diego Zoo in California. But just in case no kin turn up, the zoo hopes to add tissue from George to their Noah's Ark of cell lines, perhaps one day to clone a twin.

Giant Panda Numbers Are Surging—or Are They?

Jerry Guo
Science, **May 18, 2007**

Experts are sparring over a controversial count of wild pandas and plans to expand captive breeding of China's revered symbol

WANGLANG NATURE RESERVE, CHINA—The excited cry of a park ranger pierces the stillness of a bamboo forest high in the Min Mountains. Zhan Xiangjiang, an ecologist with the Institute of Zoology in Beijing, bounds through waist-deep snowdrifts to investigate. Catching up with the ranger, he kneels down and points at a small, round object that, at first glance, looks like a greenish yam. "Smell this!" he exclaims. The not-unpleasant odor of fresh bamboo wafts up. Along with other clues—chewed bamboo stalks, paw prints and urine-marked trees—the fresh scat is the latest evidence that Zhan's monitoring team is hot on the heels of a giant panda.

Their quarry may be elusive, but Zhan is upbeat. "Pandas are making a comeback here," he declares. In the mid-1980s, poaching and a mass bamboo die-off sent China's flagship animal into a tailspin: The country's wild panda population plummeted to about 1,200, landing the species on the endangered list. Experts decried its imminent extinction. But with a logging ban in all panda habitats since 1999, the species appears to be on the rebound.

It is a hotly debated question, however, whether panda populations are just beginning to regain lost ground or are already healthier than they have been for many years. Using DNA from hundreds of scat samples collected in Wanglang, Zhan and colleagues published a paper last year in *Current Biology* (20 June 2006) claiming that China may have 3,000 wild giant pandas—a doubling in less than a decade since the previous survey. The rosy analysis has been vigorously contested. "It frankly seems preposterous" that panda numbers have grown that rapidly, says David Garshelis, Bear Specialist Group co-chair for the World Conservation Union

(IUCN). Wanglang scientists defend their robust figure. "The situation [for pandas] has really improved," says Wanglang reserve vice-director Jiang Shiwei. "We've seen a population increase, with newborns every year."

Virtually nothing about the iconic mammal is without rancor. Another controversy swirls around China's program to breed giant pandas in captivity. Last year, the effort produced more than 30 cubs—a record—as well as the first captive released into the wild. Some conservationists say the breeding program can bolster wild populations. Others are skeptical. "The key is to protect the habitat, not reintroduce more pandas," says Lu Zhi, director of the nonprofit Conservation International's China office. "They can breed themselves, and it's a reasonable population already, so why add another flower to the garden?"

Arguable estimates

Zhan cups some scat in his bare hand and grins as it shimmers in the sunlight. "The shiny layer is mucus," he says—and it's full of DNA. To gauge how many pandas are prowling Wanglang, Zhan spent much of 2003 and 2004 combing the area for precious panda droppings. His zeal almost got him killed—in 2004, he slipped and broke his spine and had to endure a bumpy 400-kilometer ride to a hospital in Chengdu, the capital of Sichuan Province. He was not paralyzed, however, and returned to work after a 3-month-long convalescence.

Zhan's team extracted DNA from the mucus in 2005 and used genetic markers called microsatellite loci to identify individuals. Based on this DNA-fingerprinting technique, Zhan says there are at least 66 pandas in Wanglang—a big jump over the 27 estimated in the Third National Survey. That census, in 1998, employed the traditional bamboo-fragment method, which differentiates individuals by comparing the lengths of chewed bamboo in scat. Zhan argues that the bamboo fragment method's total of 1,596 pandas in China's 60 panda reserves low-balled the actual population size. "We found the population is much more than we thought in the past," says the Institute of Zoology's Wei Fuwen, senior author of the *Current Biology* paper.

In an unpublished letter to *Current Biology*, Garshelis and five colleagues expressed doubts about Zhan's analysis. "Our concern is that it's jumping the gun," says Garshelis. "They only have one data point [Wanglang], which they extrapolated to the entire range." And that data point is suspect, he says. Garshelis thinks that Wanglang simply can't support that many pandas; according to Zhan's estimate, one section of the reserve has two pandas per square kilometer—the highest recorded density for any bear species.

A population doubling at Wanglang is impossible, argues Wang Dajun, a panda researcher at Peking University, because habitat there shrank steadily until at least 1998, when the logging ban was enacted. By comparing satellite images from 1990 and 2000, Wang quantified a heavy degree of deforestation that, he says, must be harmful to pandas. Jiang agrees that habitat fragmentation imperils panda populations in smaller, isolated reserves—but not Wanglang.

The uncertainty means the giant panda will remain classified as endangered in an IUCN report slated for release later this year, the first panda update in a decade, says Garshelis. "I get the feeling the population is slowly growing," he says. "But until there's better evidence, there's certainly no reason to remove pandas from the endangered list."

Growing pains

On a single-lane dirt road winding between misty crags deep in Sichuan Province, traffic has slowed to a crawl. Hundreds of dump trucks and steamrollers are expanding the only road to Wolong Nature Reserve into a modern freeway. Conservation biologist George Schaller of the Wildlife Conservation Society in New York City was the first Westerner to study giant pandas in China when he came to Wolong, about 500 kilometers southwest of Wanglang, in 1980. Now, more than 100,000 tourists every year flock to Wolong, the country's most famous panda reserve, to see its 120 captive-bred pandas, the largest such population in the world.

More captives would be better, argues Wolong Director Zhang Hemin, who is aiming for 300 within the next decade. A population of this size, he says, could ensure the panda's survival for the next century while retaining 95 percent of its genetic diversity.

A decade ago, the captive birth of a single cub would cause a huge media sensation. Back then, if a mother bore twins, she would invariably abandon one and raise the other. In 2000, breeders figured out how to raise twins by allowing one cub at a time to stay with the mother and raising the other by hand. They frequently swap cubs so both learn survival lessons from mom. Now Wolong is trying to outdo last year's record number of births by artificial insemination.

Not everyone is handing out cigars. Lu argues that Wolong's ambitions may divert funds from conservation programs aiming to protect wild populations. "Maintaining a captive population is not cheap, so they seriously need to ask themselves why they need 300 pandas," she says.

Zhang defends the target. Wolong's goal, he says, is to introduce 10 to 20 captive pandas a year to shore up smaller wild populations. In April 2006, Wolong staff for the first time released a captive: Xiangxiang, a mild-mannered 5-year-old male. He was so badly mauled by a wild male last December that rangers had to treat him at the reserve's "panda hospital" before releasing him back into the wild. Then in late March, rangers found Xiangxiang dead; apparently he had fallen from a tree after clashes with other pandas, says Zhang. "The reintroduction program is very difficult," he admits. But he will not be deterred: Wolong plans to release another bred panda within the next 5 years.

Panda experts agree that the species needs all the help it can get. Tourism and development are nipping at the reserves. Tourists leave garbage, and villagers lay traps for game animals that inadvertently snare pandas, says Lu. Conservation International is testing a new community-based conservation model this year that will give villagers financial incentives to protect panda habitat outside the reserves. Three villages abutting Wanglang have signed on, and negotiations are under way to add 100 more sites in the next 3 years.

The central government, too, is taking action. Its Wildlife Conservation Protection Program seeks to bring 90 percent of wild pandas under the reserve system, from 75 percent today. In the 1980s, there were fewer than 20 reserves for pandas. Now there are 60. "The State Forestry Administration is putting a lot of money to set up this panda reserve network," says Wei, who notes that two or three reserves are added each year, on average.

Down from the mountain, Zhan's monitoring team encounters a pair of blue-eared pheasants, their most dramatic wildlife sighting all day. No black-and-white bamboo eaters—but that's not necessarily a bad thing, says Zhan. It means the pandas are somewhere in the highlands, deep in the bamboo forest and safe from humans for another day.

The Green Wall of China

By Jerry Guo
The Scientist, **May 2007**

With the Beijing Olympics just a year away and desert dunes now only 150 miles away from the city, officials have been dreaming big when it comes to battling legendary Chinese sandstorms in the capital and across the country's arid north. In 2001, the government approved a new phase of an $8 billion anti-desertification campaign, stretching from the capital to Inner Mongolia. The 2,800 mile shelterbelt—with 25 million hectares of trees planted and 10 million more hectares planned by 2050—has been the world's largest reforestation campaign.

Mega anti-desertification campaigns have worked in the past. The Dust Bowl of the American west in the 1930s prompted the creation of a 100 mile-wide shelterbelt that stretched from Canada to Texas. "It was very successful and did a lot for controlling erosion, providing wildlife habitat and protecting farmsteads," says James Brandle, a professor at the University of Nebraska, Lincoln.

According to a spokesperson for China's State Forestry Administration, things are on the right track: Between 1999 and 2004 (the last year data was available), 8,000 square kilometers of desert were rolled back, and 300 million tons of sand were prevented from flowing into the Yellow River. Around 2,500 square kilometers of land is lost each year to the expanding Gobi Desert. He also says by 2010, 40 percent of land currently affected by desertification will be brought under control, although he didn't say whether that land would be arable.

Still, Eugene Takle, an agricultural meteorologist at Iowa State University, says the Great Plains of the 1930s and the arid northeast of China in the new millennium are not parallels. "The 1930s were just an extreme period that hasn't been revisited," he says. "However, in China you're trying to put trees in a place that's always been the desert, so you're going uphills against nature in that one."

Others are also skeptical. Among a list of failings, a recent United Nations report criticized the "poor planting techniques and lack of maintenance" and "poor matching of species and clones to site conditions." For example, 750 miles of the Green Wall withered and died in Gansu Province when the hi-tech dune-fixing trees inadvertently sucked up too much water, says Yuanchun Shi, soil conservationist and former president of China Agricultural University. "Stressing the role of trees over grass and thickets was an arrogant and ill-thought out plan that contradicted scientific and economic rules," he adds. Countless trees were recently planted in the capital, but moths appeared out of the blue to strip their foliage and hopes for a green Olympics.

When trees do make it, Xinhua Zhou, a shelterbelt ecologist at University of Nebraska, Lincoln, points out that "farmers cut branches off trees every year to use as a replacement for coal or as wood." And despite the trees, Beijing will continue to suffer from sandstorms, says Shi, because airborne particles blow above the treeline. But Shi is quick to shrug off talks about Beijing's plights, saying a disproportionate amount of funds have gone to the capital while neglecting the rest of the 4 million square kilometer region (40 percent of the country's landmass) protected by the Green Wall. He points to simpler measures that would cost less money but be equally effective at stopping desertification, such as controlling sheep-grazing patterns.

Zhou says although the government is throwing a lot of funding toward the project, more hard science needs to be done in addition to planting the trees. "We really need to analyze the historical data on sandstorms, examine the structure of turbulence flow, and see what vegetation can minimize these sandstorms."

Bruce Wight, an agroforester at the US Department of Agriculture, says shelterbelts are normally used to stop the encroachment of the desert. He wonders about the 8,000 square kilometers of land reclaimed from desertification: "I'd be skeptical how feasible that is."

Year of the Panda

By Jerry Guo
The Scientist, **May 2007**

On a March afternoon, there are so many pandas in the "kindergarten pen" at Wolong Nature Reserve in Sichuan Province, it's hard to keep track of their antics. One is attempting a handstand while three others are playing king of the hill.

These carefree cubs—a record 19 from Wolong's 2006 breeding season—are part of the dramatic comeback for a symbol of conservation: the giant panda.

The pampered toddlers may one day follow Xiangxiang, the first captive panda released into the wild in April 2006, as part of the campaign to prop up the wild population, estimated at 1,600 in 2001. China's central government has increased the number of reserves from 13 a decade ago to 59 this year, with 2-3 coming online every year, says Wolong Director Hemin Zhang. The large number of reserves covers 50 percent of the panda's habitat and 75 percent of the population. They've also banned logging of natural forests and started a "Grain for Green" campaign to encourage farmers to restore the native habitat.

On the captive breeding front, Zhang says Wolong will soon build a new facility that can house 300 pandas, a goal that would ensure the survival of the captive population for 100 years and maintain 95 percent of its genetic diversity. "We could reach this in 8 to 10 years," he says.

As China's top panda reserve, Wolong also boasts almost 2/3 of all captive births each year thanks to their obsession with perfecting artificial insemination over the last 15 years and discovering in 2000 how to keep twins alive by removing one of them from the mother. But Zhi Lu, Conservation International's China director, isn't sharing in their joy. "They seriously need to ask themselves why they need 300 pandas, because maintaining a captive population is not cheap," she says.

The reintroduction campaign took a serious hit this past December when a rival male badly injured Xiangxiang. Because of his mild-manners from a captive upbringing, he has been having a hard time fitting in with the wild crowd. And earlier this year, rangers lost track of him when his GPS battery died. Rangers were dispatched last month in a renewed search. "If Xiangxiang dies or not, we will continue this kind of work," says Zhang. He expects more to be released in 5 years, although no plans have been made for reintroductions in the next two.

Some, however, question the need for a reintroduction component as part of captive breeding. "Why add another flower to the garden?" asks Lu. "There's a reasonable population size already in the wild."

The size of that population, it turns out, is a bit controversial. "The trend is that the pandas are coming back," says Fuwen Wei, the principal investigator behind a population study that claimed the population might be double the estimate of 1998's Third National Survey. Using DNA fingerprints collected from fresh feces, Wei was able to identify 66 individuals in a key reserve. The Third National Survey found just 27 in 1998.

That survey, however, sampled feces during a brief two-week window using the standard bamboo-fragment size method (which compares the lengths of chewed bamboo to distinguish between individuals), while Wei's study sampled feces over a period of two years. "It's like comparing how many people live in your house versus how many can fit in it," says Dave Garshelis, International Union for the Conservation of Nature and Natural Resources's bear specialist. "Frankly, their estimate seems preposterous." He says the genetic method tends to make up individuals out of thin air but the bite-size method may mistake two neighboring individuals as one, so the magic number must lie somewhere in between.

If Wei's study is correct, pandas would be off the IUCN's Red List of endangered species. Gershelis says he chose to keep the panda listed as endangered this year, the first update in more than a decade, as a precaution. "What's really happening on the ground is the population is doing very well … but to drop it off the list would make some think it's out of the woods," he says.

Dajun Wang, a panda expert at Peking University, says he believes there's closer to 28 pandas at Wanglang. He has another concern: "It's impossible to afford so many pandas," he says, because there simply isn't enough room. Right now Wang is working on a 3D stereo-imaging system that will visually identify each individual— and hopefully be more accurate than current methods. By placing three cameras in a triangle around the laser trap, he will be able to reconstruct a 3D model of each individual. "You could measure not only pandas, but other animals," he says.

"I think panda conservation is a success story, but that doesn't mean they are forever safe," says Lu. On the drive out of Wolong, what used to be a one-lane dirt road is being converted into a modern freeway to welcome with open arms the 100,000 tourists that flock to the reserve each year. Around a sharp bend, a lumbering green wholly-mammoth of a truck stacked with fresh bamboo passes by on its way to Wolong, to feed the playful cubs for another day.

Appendix C:
Science Organizations

ORGANIZATIONS OF SPECIAL NOTE

American Association for the Advancement of Science
Largest general science society in the world. Publishes *Science*; offers news, education, workshops and access to the annual meeting where top scientists meet to discuss the latest developments in science.
www.aaas.org

Association for Computing Machinery
Largest professional society for just computer scientists, mainly academics. Publishes a student journal that I run, *Crossroads*.
www.acm.org
www.acm.org/crossroads

American Junior Academy of Science
A national umbrella organization for state junior academies of science, which often offers science workshops and research opportunities for high school students.
www.amjas.org

Institute of Electrical and Electronic Engineers
Largest professional society for computer scientists and electrical engineers.
www.ieee.org

National Academy of Science
Brings together top scientists across the nation to advise the federal government on science policy, publishes a top research journal, *Proceedings of the National Academies of Science*.
www.nas.org

National Association of Science Writers
Association in which I am a student member, offers stipends to go to the annual AAAS meeting and mentorships for students interested in science journalism.
www.nasw.org

MORE ORGANIZATIONS

Academy of Organizational and Occupational Psychiatry
www.aoop.org

Air and Waste Management Association
www.awma.org

American Academy of Child and Adolescent Psychiatry
www.aacap.org

American Academy of Forensic Science
www.aafs.org

American Academy of Medical Administrators
www.aameda.org

American Association for Clinical Chemistry
www.aacc.org

American Association for Geriatric Psychiatry
www.aagpgpa.org

American Association for History and Computing
www.theaahc.org

American Association for the Advancement of Science
www.aaas.org

American Association of Anatomists
www.anatomy.org

American Association of Clinical Endocrinologists
www.aace.com

American Association of Immunologists
www.aai.org

American Association of Zoo Keepers, Inc.
www.aazk.org

American Astronomical Society
www.aas.org

American Board of Forensic Entomology
http://research.missouri.edu/entomology/

American Chemical Society
www.chemistry.org

American Counseling Association
www.counseling.org

American Crystallographic Association
http://aca.sdsc.edu

American Dietetic Association
www.eatright.org

American Fisheries Society
www.fisheries.org

American Institute of Aeronautics and Astronautics
www.aiaa.org

American Institute of Architects
www.aia.org

American Institute of Biological Sciences
www.aibs.org

American Institute of Chemists
www.theaic.org

American Institute of Physics
www.aip.org

American Mathematical Society
www.ams.org

American Medical Association
www.ama-assn.org

American Medical Directors Association
www.amda.com

American Nutraceutical Association
www.americanutra.com

American Peptide Society
www.ampepsoc.org

American Physiological Society
www.the-aps.org

American Phytopathological Society
www.apsnet.org

American Professional Practice Association
www.appa-assn.com

American Psychiatric Association
www.psych.org

American Psychoanalytic Association
www.apsa.org

American Psychological Association
www.apa.org

American Psychological Society
www.psychologicalscience.org

American Public Health Association
www.apha.org

American School Counselor Association
www.schoolcounselor.org

American Society for Biochemistry and Molecular Biology
www.asbmb.org

American Society for Bioethics and Humanities
www.asbh.org

American Society for Bone and Mineral Research
www.asbmr.org

American Society for Cell Biology
www.ascb.org

American Society for Clinical Investigation
www.asci-jci.org

American Society for Clinical Laboratory Science
www.ascls.org

American Society for Cybernetics
www.asc-cybernetics.org

American Society for Gravitational and Space Biology
http://baby.indstate.edu/asgsb/index.html

American Society for Horticultural Science
www.ashs.org

American Society for the Information Age
www.asis.org

American Society for Investigative Pathology
www.asip.org

American Society for Microbiology
www.asm.org

American Society for Nutrition
www.nutrition.org

American Society for Pharmacology and Experimental Therapeutics
www.aspet.org

American Society for Photobiology
www.pol-us.net

American Society for Virology
www.asv.org

American Society of Agronomy
www.agronomy.org

American Society of Animal Science
www.asas.org

American Society of Clinical Pathologists
www.ascp.org

American Society of Electroneurodiagnostic Technologists
www.aset.org

American Society of Human Genetics
www.ashg.org

American Society of Ichthyologists and Herpetologists
www.asih.org

American Society of Landscape Architects
www.asla.org

American Society of Limnology and Oceanography
www.aslo.org

American Society of Mammalogists
www.mammalsociety.org

American Society of Parasitologists
http://asp.unl.edu

American Society of Plant Biologists
www.aspb.org

American Society of Plant Taxonomists
www.sysbot.org

American Statistical Association
www.amstat.org

American Zoo and Aquarium Association
www.aza.org

Animal Behavior Society
www.animalbehavior.org/ABS

Association for Biology Laboratory Education
www.zoo.toronto.edu/able

Association for Computational Linguistics
www.aclweb.org

Association for Computers and the Humanities
www.ach.org

Association for Computing Machinery
www.acm.org

Association for Humanistic Psychology
www.ahpweb.org

Association for Laboratory Automation
www.labautomation.org

Association for Psychological Type
www.aptcentral.org

Association for the Advancement of Computing in Education
www.aace.org

Association for Women in Mathematics
www.awm-math.org

Association of Biomolecular Resource Facilities
www.abrf.org

Association of Energy Engineers
www.aeecenter.org

Association of Internet Technology Professionals
www.aitp.org/index.jsp

Association of Medical Illustrators
www.medical-illustrators.org

Association of Neuroscience Departments and Programs
www.andp.org

Biomedical Engineering Society
www.bmes.org

Biophysical Society
www.biophysics.org

Biotechnology Industry Organization
www.bio.org

Botanical Society of America
www.botany.org

Cognitive Science Society
www.cognitivesciencesociety.org

Computer Professionals for Social Responsibility
www.cpsr.org

Conservation International
www.conservation.org

Ecological Society of America
www.esa.org

Endocrine Society
www.endo-society.org

Engineering Society of Detroit
www.esd.org

Entomological Society of America
www.entsoc.org

Environment Protection Operation
www.e-p-o.org

Environmental Careers Organization
www.eco.org

European Federation of Biophysics
www.efb-central.org

Federation of American Societies for Experimental Biology
www.faseb.org

Genetics Society of America
www.genetics-gsa.org

IEEE Computer Society
www.genetics-gsa.org

Institute of Electrical and Electronic Engineers
www.ieee.org

Institute of Mathematical Statistics
www.imstat.org

Institute of Physics
www.iop.org

International Association for Cross-Cultural Psychology
www.iaccp.org

International Association of Mathematical Physics
www.iamp.org

International Society for Theoretical Psychology
www.udallas.edu/istp

International Society of Arboriculture
www.isa-arbor.com

International Society of Political Psychology
www.ispp.org

Marine Advanced Technology Education Center
www.marinetech.org

Marine Conservation Biology Institute
www.mcbi.org

Mathematical Association of America
www.maa.org

Microscopy Society of America
www.msa.microscopy.com

Mycological Society of America
www.erin.utoronto.ca/~w3msa

NAADAC - The Association for Addiction Professionals
www.naadac.org

National Arborist Association
www.natlarb.com

National Association for Environmental Management
www.naem.org

National Association of Biology Teachers
www.nabt.org

National Association of Cognitive and Behavioral Therapists
www.nacbt.org

National Association of Environmental Professionals
www.nacbt.org

National Association of Medical Staff Services
www.namss.org

National Association of Power Engineers
www.powerengineers.com

National Association of Professional Geriatric Care Managers
www.caremanager.org

National Association of Science Writers
www.nasw.org

National Association of Social Workers
www.naswdc.org

National Geographic Society
www.nationalgeographic.com

National Institutes of Health
www.nih.gov

National Registry of Environmental Professionals
www.nrep.org

National Science Foundation
www.nsf.gov

National Science Teachers Association
www.nsta.org

National Society of Genetic Counselors
www.nsgc.org

National Society of Professional Engineers
www.nspe.org

Natural Science Collections Alliance
www.nscalliance.org

Nature Conservancy
www.nature.org

New York Biotechnology Association
www.nyba.org

Phycological Society of America
www.psaalgae.org

Physics News, Jobs and Resources
www.physicsweb.org

Protein Society
www.proteinsociety.org

Society for a Science of Clinical Psychology
http://pantheon.yale.edu/~tat22

Society for Computers in Psychology
www.scip.ws

Society for Conservation Biology
www.conbio.org

Society for Developmental Biology
www.sdbonline.org

Society for Ecological Restoration
www.ser.org

Society for Industrial and Organizational Psychology
www.siop.org

Society for Industrial and Applied Mathematics
www.siam.org

Society for Industrial Microbiology
www.simhq.org

Society for Integrative and Comparative Biology
www.sicb.org

Society for Invertebrate Pathology
www.sipweb.org

Society for Marine Mammology
www.marinemammalogy.org

Society for Mathematical Biology
www.smb.org

Society for Modeling and Simulation International
www.scs.org

Society for Neuroscience
www.sfn.org

Society for Personality and Social Psychology
www.spsp.org

Society for Technical Communication
www.stc.org

Society for the Study of Amphibians and Reptiles
www.ukans.edu/~ssar

Society for the Study of Reproduction
www.ssr.org

Society of American Foresters
www.safnet.org

Society of Environmental Journalists
www.sej.org

Society of Mexican American Engineers and Scientists
www.maes-natl.org

Society of Wetland Scientists
www.sws.org

Society of Women Engineers
www.societyofwomenengineers.org

Tree Care Industry Association
www.natlarb.com

USENIX
www.usenix.org

World Conservation Union
www.iucn.org

World Wildlife Fund
www.worldwildlife.org

Young Mathematicians Network
www.youngmath.net

Appendix D:
Websites

College Confidential–*arguably the busiest college admissions forum*
www.collegeconfidential.com

EurekAlert!–*breaking science news, often used by journalists*
www.eurekalert.org

Google Scholars–*online search engine for research papers*
http://scholar.google.com

Reddit–*user-submitted links, often to nifty science studies*
www.reddit.com

ScienceBlogs–*a collection of great blogs on topics like biology, policy and earth sciences*
www.scienceblogs.com

ScienceDaily–*breaking news daily, gathered from press releases*
www.sciencedaily.com

ScienceForums–*a lively forum for researchers and beginners alike, with 300,000 posts so far*
www.scienceforums.net

SuperCollege–*college admissions articles and free scholarship search*
www.supercollege.com

The Science Forum–*another forum with discussions broken down by subject*
www.thescienceforum.com

Zotero–*great manager tool for research citations and sources*
www.zotero.org

Appendix E:
Free Online Course Material

AP COURSES

Course descriptions, sample test questions and links to resources.
www.collegeboard.com/student/testing/ap/subjects.html

AP Biology
Online class site, with practice tests, labs and problem sets.
www.ekcsk12.org/science/apbio/curriculum.html

AP Chemistry portal
www.shs.nebo.edu/Faculty/Haderlie/apchem/apchem.html

AP Chemistry notes
www.tvgreen.com/apchem/apnotes.htm

AP Physics Mechanics syllabus
www.intuitor.com/student/AP_MechSyl.php

FREE ONLINE COURSES FROM UNIVERSITIES

Carnegie Mellon University
www.cmu.edu/oli

Foothill De-Anza Community College District
http://sofia.fhda.edu

Johns Hopkins Bloomberg School of Public Health
http://ocw.jhsph.edu

MIT
http://ocw.mit.edu

OpenCourseWare Consortium
List of all member universities offering free courses online, including lots of international universities.
www.ocwconsortium.org

OpenCourseWare Finder
Search based on your interests. Right now hundreds of courses on endless science topics pop up.
http://opencontent.org/ocwfinder/

Tufts University
http://ocw.tufts.edu

University of California at Berkeley
http://webcast.berkeley.edu/courses.php

Utah State University
http://ocw.usu.edu

ONLINE TEXTBOOKS

Biology textbook—*popular college level text*
www.ultranet.com/~jkimball/BiologyPages/W/Welcome.html

C++ textbook
www.codeguru.com/cpp/tic/tic_c.shtml

Classic calculus textbook
http://ocw.mit.edu/ans7870/resources/Strang/strangtext.htm

Ecology textbook—*college level text from UC-Irvine*
http://darwin.bio.uci.edu/~sustain/bio65/Titlpage.htm

Economics textbooks—*from intro to advanced, including statistics textbooks*
www.oswego.edu/~economic/newbooks.htm

Genetics textbook—*intermediate college level*
www.cc.ndsu.nodak.edu/instruct/mcclean/plsc431/431g.htm

Hyperstat online statistics textbook
http://davidmlane.com/hyperstat/

Java textbook
http://math.hws.edu/javanotes/

Math textbooks—*almost 70*
www.math.gatech.edu/~cain/textbooks/onlinebooks.html

Microbiology textbook—*college level from UW-Madison*
www.bact.wisc.edu/microtextbook/index.html

Molecular biology textbook—*basic college level*
www.iacr.bbsrc.ac.uk/notebook/courses/guide/

Multivariable textbook
www.math.gatech.edu/~cain/notes/calculus.html

Online books—*including classic science manuscripts*
http://digital.library.upenn.edu/books/

Online textbook store—*billed as the largest on the web*
www.safarix.com

Physics textbook—*covers just light and matter, good AP text*
www.lightandmatter.com/area1.html

Physics textbook—*for biology and chemistry students, basic college level, U. Cincinnati*
www.rwc.uc.edu/koehler/biophys/text.html

Science textbooks—*some on general topics, others for specialty fields*
http://spot.colorado.edu/~dubin/bookmarks/b/1240.html

Appendix F:
Peer-Reviewed Journals

Cell
Lots of papers on basic research in molecular biology.
www.cell.com

Current Biology
Likes to publish catchy short research pieces, such as on tortoises and pandas.
www.current-biology.com

Nature
One of the top general science journals. Offers news, policy and reviews and publishes other journals on specific topics, such as *Nature Medicine* and *Nature Gene Therapy*.
www.nature.com

New England Journal of Medicine
Top journal on clinical and medical research.
http://content.nejm.org

Proceedings of the National Academy of Sciences
of the United States of America (PNAS)
Top general journal, includes papers on psychology, anthropology and other social sciences.
www.pnas.org

Public Library of Science
The most successful free research journal published online in areas such as biology, medicine, genetics and computational biology.
www.plos.org

Science

One of the top general science journals that offers great news (I freelance for them).
www.science.com

Appendix G:
Popular Science Publications

NEWSPAPERS

Los Angeles Times
www.latimes.com

The New York Times—*Science section*
www.nytimes.com/pages/science

Wall Street Journal (need to pay for online subscription)
www.wsj.com

MAGAZINES

American Scientist—*more research geared*
www.americanscientist.org

Discover—*geared towards kids and hot topics*
www.discovermagazine.com

Nature—*good handle on science news*
www.nature.com

New Scientist—*general science magazine, emphasis on tech*
www.newscientist.com

Popular Science—*general science, new research*
www.popsci.com

Science–*great coverage of news in the world of research*
www.science.com

Science News–*new research studies*
www.sciencenews.org

Scientific American–*great in-depth features*
www.sciam.com

Seed–*a Wired version for biologists*
www.seedmagazine.com

Technology Review–*you guessed it*
www.technologyreview.com

The Scientist–*for the professional biologist*
www.thescientist.com

Wired–*the tech magazine to read*
www.wired.com

Appendix H:
Books

Here are some great nonfiction books about science and technology, books with interesting science and great writing and material for future research projects. Some of these authors are the best writers on science of our times.

***A Brief History of Time**—astrophysics for dummies!*
Stephen Hawking

***Blink: The Power of Thinking without Thinking**—about the first two seconds of looking*
Malcolm Gladwell

***Collapse: How Societies Choose to Fail or Succeed**—gives theories for how many fabled lost civilizations collapsed*
Jared Diamond

***Earth in the Balance**—an Inconvenient Truth tale in book form*
Al Gore

***Einstein: His Life and Universe**—a look at his life outside the lab*
Walter Isaacson

***Freakonomics**—A Rogue Economist Explores the Hidden Side of Everything—layman's economics*
Steven Levitt, Stephen Dubner

***God Delusion**—science versus religion debate*
Richard Dawkins

Guns, Germs and Steel: The Fates of Human Societies—*history of societies through the eyes of an evolutionary biologist*
Jared Diamond

Happiness: A History—*you get the picture*
Darrin McMahon

How Doctors Think—*how doctors aren't as infallible as you think*
Jerome Groopman

How to Lie with Statistics—*tips on how to use statistics accurately*
Darrell Huff

Jane Goodall: The Woman Who Redfined Man—*an in-depth, new look at a famous biologist*
Dale Peterson

Man Who Mistook His Wife for a Hat—*thrilling psychological case studies*
Oliver Sacks

The Canon: A Whirligig Tour of the Beautiful Basics of Science—*fundamentals of science*
Natalie Angier

The Double Helix—*a memoir from one of the discoverers of DNA*
James Watson

Tipping Point: How Little Things Can Make a Big Difference—*social epidemics*
Malcolm Gladwell

More Great Books and Resources
from SuperCollege

Learn How to Get into
the College of Your Dreams

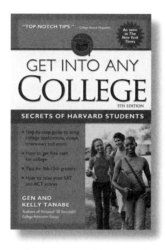

- A complete, step-by-step guide to acing college applications, essays, interviews and more

- How to get free cash for college

- Tips for 9th-12th graders

- How to raise your SAT and ACT scores

- Secrets to writing an irresistible essay

- How to create a stunning application

- Tips for mastering the interview

- Proven methods for parents to give your student an edge

Get into Any College

ISBN13: 9781932662146
ISBN: 1932662146
Price: $16.95

*Get your copy at bookstores nationwide or
from www.supercollege.com*

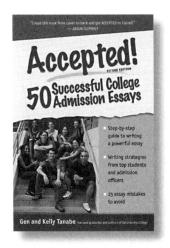

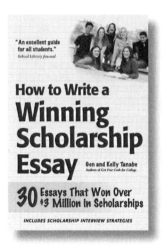

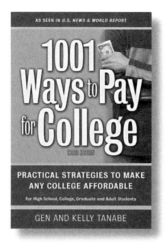

You Can Write a High Scoring Essay Even if You Hate to Write

- Learn what the SAT test graders look for when scoring an essay and how to use this to your advantage

- Master prewriting techniques, outlines and thesis statements to write higher-scoring essays

- Get insider tips from SAT graders and top tutors

- Examine over 30 sample essays with scores and commentary including how to transform low scoring essays into high scoring ones.

Ace the SAT Writing Even if You Hate to Write: Shortcuts and Strategies to Score Higher Regardless of Your Skill Level

ISBN13: 9781932662115
ISBN: 1932662111
Price: $16.95

Get your copy at bookstores nationwide or from www.supercollege.com

Get More Resources and Tools at SuperCollege.com

Visit www.supercollege.com for more free resources on scholarships, financial aid and college admissions.

About the Author

JERRY GUO has won more than $120,000 in unrestricted college scholarships, many because of his research projects in high school. His first project was to tackle the rising problem of spam. He's also worked on Galapagos giant tortoises at Yale, flower genetics at Caltech and metastatic breast cancer at the National Institutes of Health. As a senior, Jerry was selected one of the top 20 students in America by *USA Today* and top 50 volunteers by Prudential. He was a Davidson Fellow Laureate, a Siemens Competition Regional Finalist and third place divisional winner at Intel International Science Fair. Perhaps his zaniest accolade, a minor planet was recently named after him.

At Yale, he was a heavyweight rower and staff reporter covering the law school for the *Yale Daily News*. He currently serves as Editor-in-Chief of *Crossroads*, the country's largest student tech magazine, with 20,000 print subscribers. Jerry also writes for *Science* Magazine, *Nature*, *The Scientist* and *Yale Journal of Medicine and Law*, having reported from the Galapagos Islands, Costa Rica, Three Gorges Dam and Wolong Panda Reserve.

He is a member of the National Association of Science Writers, American Association for the Advancement of Science, Association for the Advancement of Artificial Intelligence, Association for Computing Machinery and Society for the Study of Amphibians and Reptiles. He loves napping, mountain biking, camping and gaming, in that order. Jerry is currently a junior majoring in economics and can be reached at jerry.guo@yale.edu.